Cambridge Elements ≡

Elements in Public and Nonprofit Administration
edited by
Andrew Whitford
University of Georgia
Robert Christensen
Brigham Young University

MANAGEMENT AND GOVERNANCE OF INTERGOVERNMENTAL ORGANIZATIONS

Ryan Federo
Universitat de les Illes Balears, Palma de Mallorca
Angel Saz-Carranza
ESADE Business School
Marc Esteve
University College London & ESADE Business School

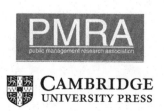

CAMBRIDGE
UNIVERSITY PRESS

University Printing House, Cambridge CB2 8BS, United Kingdom

One Liberty Plaza, 20th Floor, New York, NY 10006, USA

477 Williamstown Road, Port Melbourne, VIC 3207, Australia

314–321, 3rd Floor, Plot 3, Splendor Forum, Jasola District Centre, New Delhi – 110025, India

79 Anson Road, #06–04/06, Singapore 079906

Cambridge University Press is part of the University of Cambridge.

It furthers the University's mission by disseminating knowledge in the pursuit of education, learning, and research at the highest international levels of excellence.

www.cambridge.org
Information on this title: www.cambridge.org\9781108827591
DOI: 10.1017/9781108908283

© Ryan Federo, Angel Saz-Carranza and Marc Esteve 2020

First published 2020

A catalogue record for this publication is available from the British Library.

ISBN 978-1-108-82759-1 Paperback
ISSN 2515-4303 (online)
ISSN 2515-429X (print)

Management and Governance of Intergovernmental Organizations

Elements in Public and Nonprofit Administration

DOI: 10.1017/9781108908283
First published online: December 2020

Ryan Federo
Universitat de les Illes Balears, Palma de Mallorca

Angel Saz-Carranza
ESADE Business School

Marc Esteve
University College London & ESADE Business School

Author for correspondence: Angel Saz-Carranza, angel.saz@esade.edu

Abstract: What happens to intergovernmental organizations (IGOs) after their creation has remained in mystery over the years. Although the current globalized outlook has sparked new and growing interest in the role that IGOs play in the global landscape, the scholarship has largely focused on the political aspects of cooperation, primarily on how and why different IGO member states interact with each other and the outcomes associated with such cooperation. Research is yet to untangle how these organizations work and operate. This Element addresses this niche in the literature by delving into two important aspects: the management and governance of IGOs. We build on a four-year research program where we have collected three types of different data and produced several papers. Ultimately, the Element seeks to provide scholars with a description of the inner workings of IGOs, while providing guidance to policymakers on how to manage and govern them.

Keywords: intergovernmental organizations, strategy, board of directors, chief executives, governance

ISBNs: 9781108827591 (PB), 9781108908283 (OC)
ISSNs: 2515–4303 (online), 2515-429X (print)

Contents

1 Introduction

With the current globalized outlook, intergovernmental organizations (IGOs) have become fundamental to solving complex policy problems across the world. These organizations, established by member states to promote international cooperation, are used to manage the delivery of global public goods (Federo and Saz-Carranza 2018). Research has long underscored the importance of IGOs in governing and shaping the institutional environments in which firms, national governments, public entities, and nonprofit organizations operate (e.g., Bach and Newman 2014; Shaffer 2015). However, most studies have focused on the political aspects of cooperation, in particular, how and why various member states interact, and the outcomes associated with cooperation. Although IGOs are "organizations," operating within the same bureaucratic system that underpins businesse, public agencies, and nonprofit entities, few studies have offered a holistic understanding of the way in which IGOs function and operate, particularly accounting for their differences in leadership and governance structures. This Element addresses such a gap in the literature and investigates what happens to IGOs after they are created. It does so by delving deeply into two important areas: the management and governance of IGOs. It provides scholars and managers with a detailed description of the differences in IGOs and their inner workings, while offering practical guidance on how to manage and govern them effectively.

To explain how IGOs are managed and governed, this study builds on a four-year research program that collected three different types of data and produced several academic papers. Data related to the performance and governance of international development IGOs make it possible to identify governance structures that characterize high-performing IGOs (see Federo and Saz-Carranza 2018, 2020). A second dataset, detailing the organizational and governance characteristics of all global IGOs (sixty-nine in total), reveals which organizational characteristics are linked to particular governance structures in IGOs. Finally, qualitative data on the chief executives of IGO secretariats show how they set strategies and interact with members and boards (see Saz-Carranza 2015). This Element identifies and explores the leadership and governance structures and practices that lead to agreements between members and chief executives, enabling IGOs to create and implement strategies.

The succeeding parts of the Element are divided into four sections. Section 2 uses a "borrowing approach" to explain how various management theories, drawn from the for-profit, public, and nonprofit literature, can be used to understand IGOs (Federo 2017). Section 3 discusses the management of IGOs by examining how IGO leaders shape and direct their respective organizations (Saz-Carranza 2015) and theorizing how IGOs can use strategy as a tool to craft organizational goals and objectives, which could be a way of orienting organizations (Federo and Saz-Carranza 2017). Section 4 investigates the governance of IGOs, particularly focusing on how IGO chief executives are chosen (Saz-Carranza et al. 2018) and how IGO boards participate in strategy making (Federo and Saz-Carranza, 2018) and perform their monitoring function (Federo and Saz-Carranza, 2020). The final section concludes with this Element's theoretical implications that can inform future research, while offering practitioners valuable managerial insights to improve IGO outcomes.

2 IGOs as Organizations

The first section uses a "borrowing approach" to show how various management theories related to for-profit, public, and nonprofit organizations can be used to analyze and understand IGOs. Traditional approaches within the international relations (IR) literature straddle the functionalist-constructivist divide. The functionalist approach assumes that IGOs are independent entities, established by interdependently integrated state actors. These actors promote cooperation in order to pursue collective interests; they are capable of influencing global policies, as well as state preferences and behavior (Mitrany 1948). In its central premise, the functionalist approach focuses on incentives that prompt actors to solve cooperation problems efficiently, explaining why, when, and how state actors delegate specific tasks to IGOs (Simmons 2008). By contrast, the constructivist approach aims to understand the goals and intentions of state actors that create IGOs (Ruggie 1982). State actors interact with other actors in the international arena. They create socially constructed realities by defining meanings, norms of good behavior, the nature of social actors, and legitimate forms of social action (e.g., Barnett and Finnemore 1999, 2004; Hawkins and Jacoby 2006). The constructivist approach highlights the importance of international legitimacy, driven by political and social purposes (Simmons 2008). The functionalist and constructivist approaches have both primarily explained the organizational design of IGOs. Neither approach has explored the organizational-performance implications of IGO organizational design (Federo 2017).

As Ness and Brechin (1988) have noted, IGOs are characterized by self-sufficient bureaucratic structures that allow them to function at will. This Element moves beyond traditional IR approaches, drawing on organization theories from the management literature to understand how IGO organizational performance can be strengthened through good management and governance.

In doing so, it highlights a range of theories, including agency, resource dependence, stakeholder, and institutional theory.

As IGOs become autonomous organizational actors, able to participate in international forums, influence state behavior, and initiate collective actions, they also become goal-directed entities structured to operate, choose their own direction, and survive. However, their autonomy is restricted by the vested mandate and delegated authority of the member states that established them. Increasingly, scholars have begun to draw on agency theory to explain an agency problem that arises when IGOs exploit their autonomy and deviate from the expectations of member states (e.g., Hawkins et al. 2006; Nielson and Tierney 2003). Agency problems occur when agents are incentivized and guided by self-interest and managerial opportunism to make decisions or to pursue goals that do not align with those of principals, adversely affecting them (Eisenhardt 1989; Jensen and Meckling 1976). In common with agency theory, this Element assumes that boards of directors (e.g., John and Senbet 1998) and approaches designed to align the strategies of agents and principals (e.g., Westphal and Fredrickson 2001) can act as efficient mechanisms to reduce IGO agency problems.

Alongside the incentive logic assumed in agency theory, the logic of abilities proposed in resource dependence theory (RDT) provides another important way of understanding organizations. A resource dependence approach assumes that organizations are open systems influenced by contingencies related to the external environment (Pfeffer and Salancik 1978). The main tenet of RDT involves minimizing external dependencies to reduce the uncertainty and transaction costs associated with external contingencies. As IGOs, by their nature, depend on the external environment, RDT can help to explain how they manage external contingencies that influence their goals and inner workings. For instance, IGO executives and boards of directors can provide resources to promote strategy making. Thus, integrating the logics of incentives (agency theory) and abilities (RDT) offers a holistic view of organizational designs, structures, behaviors, and outcomes (e.g., Hillman and Dalziel 2003; Boivie et al. 2016).

It is another prominent feature of IGOs that their activities are influenced by the multiple, and often conflicting, needs and expectations of a wide array of stakeholders. Stakeholders are individuals or organizations that affect, or are affected by, the actions of an organization (Freeman 1984). In addition to the member states that establish IGOs and the staff members who make them function, stakeholders include other IGOs, nongovernmental organizations (NGOs), the business sector, and the general public across transnational borders. Some stakeholders are not relevant to an IGO's activities. This Element proposes building on stakeholder theory to identify salient stakeholders who can influence an IGO's activities and functioning.

In a context characterized by the expectations of multiple stakeholders, legitimacy becomes an important consideration. Intergovernmental organizations do not operate within an overarching national jurisdiction or a formalized institutional framework; their legitimacy transcends any formalized structure. In effect, it rises above the member states, anchored by various forces in the internal and external environment. In the management literature, institutional theory has taken the lead in explaining how organizations survive when their operations conform to prescribed, socially legitimate behaviors (Meyer and Rowan 1977). To understand the association between such behaviors and a range of IGO design-related and strategic choices, institutional theory is used to explore how legitimacy works in IGOs, in line with a growing IR literature (e.g., Coicaud and Heiskanen 2001; Tallberg and Zurn 2019).

In recent years, the organization theories that dominate management research have increasingly complemented existing IR approaches, resulting in a fuller understanding of IGOs. Many scholars now use agency theory to understand IGO delegation, resource dependence theory to explore IGO resourcing, stakeholder theory to identify actors who influence IGOs, and institutional theory to investigate IGO legitimacy. This Element combines all of these theories to achieve a holistic understanding of the ways in which IGOs can be managed and governed strategically to improve organizational outcomes.

3 Management of IGOs

This section explores how IGOs are managed, particularly focusing on how the top leadership in IGOs shape and direct their respective organizations. In the first part of the section, we focus on IGO chief executives, considering the nature of effective leadership and how executives are selected by their respective organizations. This study uses the terms "IGO leader" and "IGO chief/top executive" as synonyms. In the latter part of the section, we shift our focus to how IGO strategies are made, which indicate the direction of the organizations.

3.1 Approaches to Understanding IGO Leadership

Understanding executive leadership in multilateral organizations is crucial if the global governance system is to function adequately. The way an IGO functions depends in part on how its chief executive behaves, especially vis-à-vis the member states that established it; it also depends on the practices adopted by its top executive. Few studies have attempted to understand how such leadership figures act (the related literature includes historical, biographical works by a few former chief executives of renowned UN and Bretton Woods institutions (Boughton 2001; Kille 2006; Kraske et al. 1996). Although there are scholarly studies of heads of states and their IGO-related foreign policies (e.g., Nye 2013), little is known about the individual behavior of IGO top executives, beyond a few biographical studies of UN Secretary Generals and World Bank Presidents. This Element therefore examines the behavior of IGO chief executives. At this level of analysis, we follow Northouse (2010) in defining leadership as "a process whereby an individual influences a group of individuals to achieve a common goal" (p. 3).

3.1.1 Agency Problems with IGO Executives

To understand the roles and functions of IGO executives, agency theory has been frequently used to conceptualize the relationship between IGO chief executives and member states (Hawkins et al. 2006). Agency theory assumes that principals (i.e., members) have clear and ranked preferences, while agents (i.e., executive leaders) are strategic actors who try to substitute their own preferences for those of the principals. The principals must balance the trade-off between the cost of monitoring and aligning agents and the cost associated with strategic gaming by agents. Traditionally, agency theory conceptualizes the principal-agent relationship as conflictive.

However, bounded rationality (common to all organizational actors) combined with the assumption that IGO principals (multiple sovereign member states engaging in politics) are collective in nature, calls for a relaxation of the premise that the preferences of principals are clear and ordered. This combination, compounded by the argument that agents do not necessarily nor solely behave strategically and narrowly to advance their own self-interest, requires a better conceptualization and understanding of executive leadership.

As Hawkins et al. (2006) have noted, an agency approach to IGO delegation assumes that agents enjoy autonomy and discretion. It is precisely the question of how agents use their discretion and autonomy that interests researchers investigating IGO leadership. Agency theory has been applied to corporate governance for several decades (Fama and Jensen 1983) and to the member state/IGO relationship more recently (Hawkins et al. 2006). Agency theory assumes that principal and agent are both self-interested, bringing their goals partially into conflict (Eisenhardt 1989). The contract that binds the agent and principal together is thus the central focus. However, it is impossible to design complete contracts under conditions of bounded rationality and uncertainty (Simon 1948; Williamson 1979). In particular, it is difficult to monitor performance in the policy fields in which IGOs operate because the agent's specialization exacerbates the information asymmetry between principal and agent (Hawkins et al. 2006; Kiewiet and McCubbins 1991).

As IGO principals are collective in nature, traditional agency theory is more challenging for IGOs, given the diverse and often conflicting preferences and goals of member states. Moreover, complex principals only increase the autonomy of agents, who can play one member state against another (Lyne et al. 2006). Unanimous-decision rules, which are common in IGOs, give agents more autonomy, as principals struggle to agree on detailed and binding monitoring mechanisms produced by IGO chief executives (Hawkins et al. 2006). This Element explores the specific leadership practices adopted by IGO chief executives.

3.1.2 IGO Executives as Goal-Directed Network Leaders

An alternative approach to understanding IGO leadership draws on the literature on goal-directed networks, which include IGOs. We argue that these interorganizational collaborative contexts imply a diffuse and varying concept of the leader-follower relationship, in which there is no clear hierarchical authority between the leader and the follower. In such circumstances, leadership behaviors tend to be categorized as relational behaviors. We refer to this literature because the nonhierarchical relationship between an IGO chief executive and member states is similar to that of a network broker (i.e., leader) and organization members. The received knowledge on network leadership may provide a useful starting point for exploring the behavior of IGO leaders in relation to member-state representatives.

The term "network" is not used as a metaphor (opposed to hierarchy or market) or as a sociological model (as in "social-network analysis"), but rather to define a goal-directed interorganizational phenomenon (Isett et al. 2011; Saz-Carranza et al. 2020). Following Provan and Kenis (2008), we define goal-directed networks as "groups of three or more legally autonomous organizations that work together to achieve not only their own goals but also a collective goal." Like network members, IGO member states are simultaneously resource-interdependent and legally sovereign, making the network perspective intuitively useful.

Precisely because leadership behaviors are contingent on the amount of power held by a leader (French and Raven 1959; Northouse 2010) who lacks authority over IGO members, the goal-directed network leadership model may fit IGO leadership. Leaders of IGOs have little (if any) formal authority over member states. Goal-directed network brokers, similarly, have no formal authority over network members. This study uses the terms "network leader" and "network broker" as synonyms.

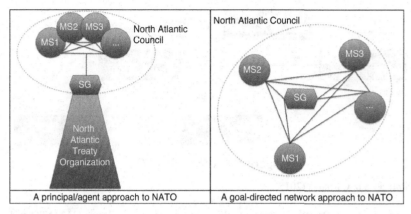

| A principal/agent approach to NATO | A goal-directed network approach to NATO |

Figure 1 Two approaches to the relationship between secretary general and member states in NATO

Source: Saz-Carranza (2015).

We argue that a network-leadership approach to IGO leadership complements – rather than contradicts – the relaxed principal/agent characterization of the IGO member states/executive leadership relationship. Figure 1 illustrates how the NATO Council can be seen as a network.

3.2 IGO Network-Leadership Practices

In exploring the topic of IGO leadership practices, two historically relevant cases illustrate the way in which IGO chief executives and their personal teams have directed the leadership practices of first, NATO, as the Secretary General during the organization's first post–Cold War enlargement process in the east, and second, the European Union, while serving as the EU High Representative during the institutional creation of the European Union's Common Foreign and Security Policy (EU-CFSP). Although the two cases involve clearly distinct contexts, both are considered successful cases of IGO leadership.

In the first case, the Secretary General of NATO successfully led the eastward expansion of IGOs, which took place between 1995 and 1999. The expansion involved two central issues that had to be resolved. First, members had to agree on which countries would join NATO during the first post–Cold War expansion. There were five candidates: the Czech Republic, Poland, Hungary, Romania, and Slovenia. The second major issue was how NATO should proceed in relation to Russia, which has never wanted NATO too close to its borders (as the ongoing Ukraine crisis reminds us). In relation to both issues, the Secretary General had to promote unity and support among member states, helping them choose new member states while simultaneously signing a partnership

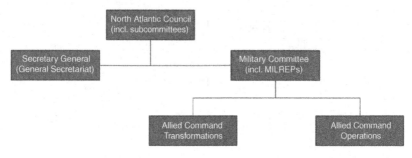

Figure 2 Structure of NATO

Source: Saz-Carranza (2015).

agreement with Russia. His major achievements were as follows: (1) NATO and Russia signed the Founding Act in May 1997; and (2) the Czech Republic, Hungary, and Poland formally joined NATO in March 1999. Figure 2 shows how NATO is structured.

The second case explores how the High Representative/Vice President (HR/ VP) of the EU-CFSP institutionally developed an intergovernmental initiative between 1999 and 2009. Here, the issue revolved around how to create a supranational institutional framework from scratch in a sector considered crucial to state sovereignty, at a moment when support for transnational institutions was beginning to stall. Given this context, the High Representative had to be capable of collectively engaging with members and persuading member states to support specific courses of action within the new collective endeavor, as well as establishing the necessary institutional structure. As the European Union began to incorporate a foreign policy, the High Representative was actively involved in designing and implementing a military structure within an IGO (the European Union) that had pacifism coded into its DNA. Figure 3 shows how the EU-CFSP is structured.

Although network leadership is similar to traditional intra-organizational leadership, it tends to focus on people-oriented behavior – creating a common vision to generate sufficient buy-in and secure resources – rather than task-related behaviors. When Silvia and McGuire (2010) surveyed 417 network leaders, they found that network leadership overlapped with intra-organizational leadership, but involved more people-oriented behavior. Although network leadership produces the same types of behavior as intra-organizational leadership, it relies more heavily on people-oriented behaviors (Silvia and McGuire 2010; Northouse 2010) and soft power (Nye 2013) to achieve collective goals. Over the past decade, network-leadership research has identified a consistent set of practices implemented by network leaders

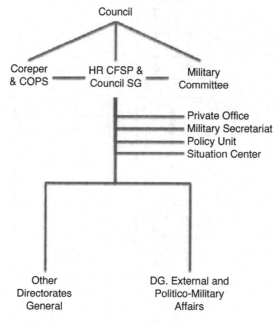

Figure 3 Structure of the EU-CFSP in 2002

Source: Saz-Carranza (2015).

(Agranoff and McGuire 2001; Huxham and Vangen 2005; Kickert et al. 1997).

3.2.1 Framing: Agent, Broker, or Both?

Framing is a key network-leadership practice aimed at generating a common vision and shared goals (Agranoff and McGuire 2001; Huxham and Vangen 2005; Kickert et al. 1997; Müller-Seitz 2012; Ospina and Saz-Carranza 2010). Networks bring together members with different frames of reference, rendering formalized and rational decision-making rules less effective (Salancik and Pfeffer 1974). The WTO, for example, has proved incapable of reaching new trade agreements, due to conflicting interests and principles, such as whether developing member states can subsidize rural farmers. Actors in a network have distinct mental frames of reference. To make joint decisions and solve social problems, they must find ways of mutually adjusting their perceptions. Framing is thus an important unifying practice.

As our qualitative data reveal, an IGO executive and members must engage in an interactive and dynamic process to define specific courses of action, goals, and strategies. The data reveal a blurry and fuzzy distinction between the agent and principal (the member states collectively) in setting courses of action. At times, the

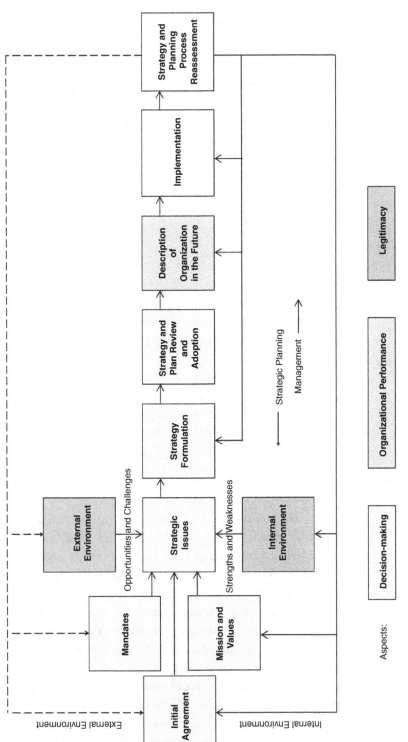

Figure 4 Strategy change cycle

Source: Federo and Saz-Carranza (2017), adapted from Bryson (2011).

executive resembles a network leader working to frame a vision and supporting strategy development, while recognizing the role of member states as principals. The executive is well aware that member states are the principals. In the case of the EU-CFSP, the High Representative's Chief of Staff recalled: "The first truly brilliant decision he made was ... [becoming] aware that ... behaving like a [European] Secretary of State ... would never work [56-EM-EU]." The executive understood that the High Representative (HR) could not treat member-state foreign services as subordinate units under his authority. As the HR himself commented: "Being at the service of the institution means convincing those who hold the power, staying one step ahead, a small step and not 20 kilometers in front because then you become irrelevant [5-JS-EU]." He referred to member states as "those who hold the power." In noting the importance of being "one step ahead," he highlighted the proactive role of the executive in framing a common vision and strategy for member states.

The HR Communication Director has described the process through which two contradictory poles (recognizing the member states as principals in charge, while simultaneously playing a major role in framing and strategizing) are combined in practice:

> There's a consultative element [in] intergovernmental policy [. . .] and there is a non-consultative element – you can't be consulting at every moment. But, if you have extremely up-to-date information about the different countries' positions [. . .] you already know [. . .] on what issues you'll act and on which you won't as well as on how far you can go.
>
> Obtaining mandates was very important, because if you were given a mandate, you were somehow on the frontline [. . .] Normally, you weren't given a mandate if you didn't seek it out [T]he objective then [. . .] was to put proposals on the table for a European policy.
>
> We sought mandates from the European Council this way [. . .] That meant having to develop complicity with the Presidency [. . .] the rotating' presidency's joint work which had to help for mandates. You thus had to be subtle so that the minister in charge felt comfortable [. . .] In other words, it was a very sophisticated circle [63/5-CG-EU].

While the EU-CFSP, like NATO, had a grand vision and a mission, these had to be encapsulated within specific and concrete actions that the members would accept and support.

> Solana realized he was becoming a political mediator – he's very good at it – and then he was capable of dragging the European Union member states with him – and, at times, putting soldiers into play, at other times judges, at other moments prison guards, other times customs agents, whatever was needed in

each specific moment – because [the European Union] was beginning to be on the map [48-EM-EU].

Unlike NATO, the EU-CFSP was new; it was obvious that stakeholders had to contribute to setting a direction. However, the NATO executive was also very proactive in fine-tuning the enlargement strategy by calling for an agreement with Russia. As the NATO Secretary General recalled: "I argued that we had to do something to reach an understanding with Russia. We had to explain it to them and reach some type of agreement [103-JS-NATO]." This comment underscores the way in which the Secretary General proposed and supported a specific course of action. In this way, IGO leaders play a key role in collectively framing a vision and setting strategy. The void that exists beneath the IGO vision or strategic goal is filled by the IGO leader, who proposes a specific course of action to the council and then executes it once an agreement is reached.

3.2.2 Communicating with Members and Facilitating their Interaction

For the European Union, given the novelty of its intergovernmental endeavor, it was extremely important to establish an appropriate operating structure that allowed it to manage members upwards. Interestingly, the HR focused on structures that allowed him to align and communicate with members, in addition to operative structures.

The structures (both procedures and organizational processes) established to enable communication with members were both formal and informal. In both cases, it was essential to maintain proper and frequent channels of communication with members. One important initial priority was to establish the formal structure of the CFSP. During the first semester after his appointment, the HR worked with the European Union's rotating presidency to set up a permanent committee – the Political and Security Committee (COPS) – separate from the permanent council committee (Permanent Representatives Committee [COREPER]). These decisions were formally taken by the council but were strongly advocated for by the High Representative. As he recalled:

> The problem was that there was no degree of trust in the discussions within COREPER: Everything was leaked out. The first doubt, consequently, was creating a permanent representation, COPS, or abandoning COREPER. To me, the most reasonable thing would have been a permanent representation to be able to face any crisis or emergency situation [17/8-JS-EU].

While NATO did not create any formal governance structures during the period studied, the Secretary General's team was very sanguine about its rigorous and formal procedures for keeping the council informed during the negotiations with Russia. As the Chief of Staff recalled:

> After each session with the Russians, the Secretary General immediately informed the Council about the results and distributed the document for the states to give their opinions, "this yes" and "that no." And that's how it worked during, I think, 106 sessions [...] And that worked, it worked, and was important because there was a meeting and always super-detailed minutes [...] We often wrote up those minutes on the plane, returning at dawn or whenever, so that the states would have them the following morning. All ambassadors received the minutes at the same time; there was no type of preference or favoritism towards the United States [116/9-JD-NATO].

Informal, multiple, and indirect channels of communication with principals became paramount in both the European Union and NATO. As the HR's Chief of Staff recounted:

> The first thing Solana did was tell everyone in the [newly created] Policy Unit that, "you're my link with your government, with your Minister of Foreign Affairs." You say that to any diplomat ... and they'll be charmed ... It transforms an analyst into a political liaison, a source of information about everything the different governments do, a collaborator between him and another minister [2-EM-EU].

Javier Solana used a unit designed for analysis and planning to additionally provide a second channel of communication with members. In a similar way, he used the Military Committee (MilCom) chair, whose formal role was simply to advise the HR, to build a common strategy (the MilCom was ultimately responsible for making military decisions). Importantly, the HR has no authority over the MilCom or its chair. As Solana's Chief of Staff recalled:

> "You are my military adviser. In principle, you'll have lunch with me every week, you'll have to give me your advice, and we'll share our thoughts." That's the type of leadership Solana exercises, he wins over the Chair of the Military Committee. The latter begins to be the conveyor belt for political ideas, and, since the Military Committee is the one that decides and makes the military decisions, the European Union follows its path [7-EM-EU].

Even the NATO executive engaged in informal relational activities to align the members and advance toward agreements. As the Secretary General's Chief of Staff recalled:

> [He built] contacts in every capital, nurturing relations with the governments, prime ministers and presidents and heads of state. He knows how to listen [and is] very receptive to opinions from members ... He avoided being

identified with a specific group of countries, whether big or small, from the East or West, and had a knack for absorbing information [122-JD-NATO].

3.2.3 Facilitating Unity

Facilitation (Klijn 2004) and synthesizing (Agranoff and McGuire 2001) are the quintessential practices used to communicate with and align network members (Müller-Seitz 2012). Facilitation eases interactions among diverse participants. Specific organizational rules play an important role in communicating with members and aligning them with collective goals. Intergovernmental organizations must create the necessary network infrastructures, formal and informal communication channels, and proper interaction procedures.

The NATO case provides a rare glimpse into the efforts of an IGO executive and the closure of decision-making through unanimity during summits, when the National Atlantic Council convenes member heads of states. The NATO Secretary General described the summit in March 1999, where the Czech Republic, Hungary, and Poland were accepted as new NATO members.

> France and Italy were very keen on Romania joining. [They were] interested in others joining besides the three German "classics." Consequently, the fight during that entire session was if those three entered or if Romania did as well [88-JS-NATO]. The meeting dragged on [90-JS-NATO].
>
> I said: "I'm going to present a proposal in two minutes, and it's going to be the definitive one. I won't allow any more debate." I took a leap then without consulting anyone … I read the meeting's conclusions in which we only accepted Hungary, the Czech Republic and Poland to join. I didn't even allow for a vote. I took the microphone and said, "the motion is passed" [84/5-JS-NATO].

The passage above illustrates two points: first, that it is necessary to allow sufficient time and space for discussion. Second, after allowing dissenting members to make their case, it is sometimes necessary to call for a decision that may not satisfy them.

3.2.4 Mobilizing Support

Mobilization, probably the best-known of these practices, captures the resources and support that networks need. Mobilization essentially builds network power by securing resources, external legitimacy, knowledge, and access from the network's external domain; it also builds support and commitment among network members.

The EU foreign affairs and security strategy required US acceptance, if all council members were to adopt the strategy. As the HR recalled:

It took many trips to Paris, London and the United States. NATO's break-up was the US's biggest fear. They were afraid of a European lobby within NATO and that NATO would somehow break up. I always had to talk with them to convince them [the US] that that wasn't going to happen [9-JS-EU].

Internal resources and support were also crucial. The HR described how the EU-CFSP set up an intelligence center, called the Situation Center, with a few key intelligence officers seconded from the intelligence services of a handful of member states:

I picked the team after talking with the most powerful countries' intelligence services. The first fight was due to not all of them being present, rather, just a few – the more powerful ones in terms of intelligence didn't want to share what they knew with the least powerful ones – and I chose those few. I named a wonderful Englishman to lead this unit [3-JS-EU].

In the case of NATO, it was equally important to generate internal support and resources. For example, US support made it possible for NATO to embark on negotiations with Russia. Had the US not refused to talk directly with Russia about this issue, Russia would never have negotiated with NATO. As the Secretary General recalled:

Strobe Talbot, number two to then US Secretary of State, Madeleine Albright, was who told Solana that he had to negotiate with Russia, not the US, fearing that bilateral negotiations would delegitimize NATO [97-JS-NATO].

3.2.5 Lessons From IGO Leadership

In addition to providing detailed accounts of how IGO executive officers experienced leadership, this section contributes to a better understanding of how IGO executives use their discretion as agents of the collective principal. Our findings suggest a more nuanced and relaxed usage of the principal-agent model (Hawkins et al. 2006) and complement this with behavior-based and experiential accounts of executive leadership. Breaking with the tenets of agency theory, IGO leaders do not maintain conflicting relationships with principals, but instead sustain a collaborative stance. The IGO leader effectively brokers and leads multiple principals as a network.

In particular, an important implication is that effective IGO executives conceive themselves – and are recognized by members – as brokers rather than subordinate agents. As such, IGO executives must help frame the institutional vision, set the goals, and select strategies. Our findings show that IGO executives frame the vision and goals and strategize (Bryson 2011; Saz-Carranza 2012). It is particularly interesting to find that IGO leaders are highly involved in developing strategies to achieve the collective vision. Collective principals generally unite around a grand agreement or general mandate, even without a shared or specific mid-term course of action. The void between vision and action is filled by executives. This pattern is particularly visible in the EU-CFSP, probably because this intergovernmental effort is relatively new, offering more space to frame a grand vision.

Another important implication is that effective IGO executives actively facilitate member interaction, both with formal and informal processes and structures (Agranoff 2007; Stcijn and Klijn 2008). A central practice among executives involves establishing formal structures and processes to keep members well informed and communicating. The EU-CFSP Chief Executive used formal structures intended for planning and analysis (seconded personnel from member-state ministries) as secondary informal channels for communicating with members. Essentially, the aim is to set up multiple channels of communication between the executive and members (Saz-Carranza 2012).

Informal ways of facilitating and communicating with members confirm recent scholarship on the informal dimension of global governance (Stone 2013). However, that emerging literature mainly remains at the state level of analysis, rather than focusing on individuals (Chwieroth 2012; Tallberg 2010).

Informal and one-on-one communication with members enables IGO leaders to understand the preferences of different members and to broker agreements more effectively (Tallberg 2004). To reach closure on decisions, in situations that involve diverse preferences, leaders must distinguish between nonnegotiable and negotiable objections. In the latter case, they must give divergent members enough space to "voice" their objections (Hirschman 1970). Their opinions on negotiable matters may be sufficient to enable consensus, avoiding an "exit" (Hirschman 1970). While IGO abandonment is uncommon (Pevehouse et al. 2004), blockage via vetoing does occur. Hence, another implication of our findings is that effective IGO executives strategically allow for nonconforming members to "voice" their opposition while simultaneously closing in on consensus.

In both cases, our findings show that the way in which an IGO leader mobilizes external and internal support conforms to RDT (e.g., Hillman et al. 2009). In the EU-CFSP case, the informal acquiescence of the United States was an essential need. Internal resources, such as key-member support, were important in both cases. However, in the EU-CFSP case, other resources, including intelligence, had to be assured by creating adequate structures that fit with the overall organizational design. Thus, IGO executives actively mobilize resources for the IGO.

3.3 Strategy Making in IGOs

Over the last few years, several IGOs have developed strategic plans to define their goals and objectives. Examples of long-term strategic plans are available publicly from many organizations, including the World Bank (WB), International Monetary Fund (IMF), International Maritime Organization (IMO), and World Health Organization (WHO). In a recent study, George, Monster, and Walker (2019) carried out a meta-analysis of the relationship between strategic planning and organizational performance in public- and private-sector organizations. Their research offers a valuable lesson: strategic planning clearly improves organizational performance. Two caveats apply, however. First, strategic planning is particularly helpful when organizational performance is measured as effectiveness (i.e., the extent to which organizations successfully achieve their goals), but it may not lead to efficiency gains. Second, strategic planning has a stronger effect on organizational performance when the strategy is formalized; thus, an organization must explicitly define its mission, vision, goals, and objectives. Given these findings, strategic planning should make an important impact on IGO performance. However – and quite surprisingly – few studies have investigated the relationship between strategy and IGOs. This section analyzes the importance of strategy, investigating how IGO managers can use strategic planning as a useful tool, crafting organizational goals and objectives to orient organizations.

Strategic planning has been defined in multiple ways. This Element uses the conceptualization proposed by Bryson (2011), who describes strategic planning as "a deliberative, disciplined effort to produce fundamental decisions and actions that shape and guide what an organization is, what it does, and why it does it" (pp. 7–8). Multiple theoretical frameworks link strategy and organizational performance. The three main frameworks identified by George, Monster, and Walker (2019) are the Harvard policy model, synoptic planning theory, and goal-setting theory. According to these authors, "the Harvard policy model argues that organizational success is contingent on the extent to which there is a fit between the organization and its environment, which can be established using tools such as SWOT (strengths, weaknesses, opportunities, and threats) analysis" (p. 3). Synoptic planning theory argues that an analytical approach to strategy making, driven primarily by a rational analysis of an organization's strengths and weaknesses, generally provides better results than a more intuitive managerial style (see Dror 1983). According to goal-setting theory, clear goals help managers decide how to allocate resources to maximize organizational priorities (see Locke and Latham 2002).

Despite the positive effect of strategic planning on organizational performance, our studies show that a number of IGOs do not use it (Federo and Saz-Carranza 2015). This section builds on our recent work on IGO strategic planning to investigate specific strategies that IGOs can use to improve their performance. The following subsections first delve into organizational design characteristics to better understand how strategic planning in IGOs differs from traditional approaches developed by general management scholars. Second, they identify management strategies that are particularly well-suited to the organizational characteristics of IGOs.

3.3.1 The Organizational Characteristics of IGOs

Volgy and colleagues have defined IGOs as "entities created with sufficient organizational structure and autonomy to provide formal, ongoing, multilateral processes of decision making between states, along with the capacity to execute the collective will of their member (states)" (2008, p. 851). Koremenos, Lipson, and Snidal (2001) have argued that the institutional design of an IGO must reflect the organizational goals it seeks to achieve. To understand the organizational design choices that differentiate IGOs from more traditional organizations, we have developed a framework, based on three main characteristics of the design-making process shown in Figure 1: decision-making, organizational performance, and legitimacy (see also Federo and Saz-Carranza 2017).

Decision-Making

The most fundamental aspect of strategic planning is probably the need to decide among several available objectives, and to select the means of achieving them. According to Ackoff, "the principal complexity in planning derives from the interrelatedness of decisions rather than from the decisions themselves" (1970, p. 3). Mintzberg (1973) has argued that the manager or management team must, as one of its core functions and responsibilities, analyze both external and internal organizational factors and choose the strategy most likely to achieve desired goals from among various alternatives. The way in which public managers select goals and actions is thus a vital part of the strategy-making process (Boyne and Walker 2004).

Organizational Performance

Organizational performance represents the light at the end of the tunnel. When managers design strategic plans, optimal organizational performance is their ultimate goal. Bryson and Roering (1987) place organizational performance at the center of every strategic plan, providing a foundation for managerial actions designed to improve an organization's performance. For strategic-planning researchers, organizational performance is the ultimate dependent variable to strive to explain (Richard et al., 2009).

Despite the importance of this concept, the organizational-performance literature has not been able to agree on a single definition of the term. Organizational performance has many meanings. To some public managers, it signifies efficiency; to others, it means service or program quality. Walker et al. (2013) have acknowledged the multidimensionality of performance and the resulting operational challenges that arise when it has to be measured. In their view, performance resembles many measures, including quality, efficiency, effectiveness, equity, probity, and responsiveness in delivering a public service. When it comes to IGOs, most classic measures of organizational performance do not apply.

As discussed in a previous study (Federo and Saz-Carranza 2017), IGOs should consider two main characteristics when defining their performance objectives. The first characteristic is the scope of the organization's proposed activities. The scope of performance measures for an international financial institution, such as the WB, differs greatly from that of an IGO that aims to promote peace in various parts of the world, such as NATO. The second characteristic refers to centralization. It is fundamental to consider the extent to which IGOs perform various tasks that are not limited to policymaking, enforcement, and information sharing. The concept of centralization refers to an IGO's overall activities, which can range from multiple activities with little connection between them (in a highly decentralized IGO) to a single activity (in a highly centralized IGO). Other authors have similarly discussed mandate-related differences, pointing out multiple conceptualizations of the term "performance" that coexist in the realm of IGOs (see, for example, Boehmer, Gartzke, and Nordstrom 2004). The scope and the degree of centralization determined by an IGO's mandate shape its targeted organizational performance.

Legitimacy

The concept of legitimacy has fewer interpretations than the concept of organizational performance. Suchman defines it as "a generalized perception or assumption that the actions of an entity are desirable, proper or appropriate within some socially constructed systems of norms, values, beliefs and definitions" (1995, p. 574). As a prominent topic in management research, legitimacy has received considerable attention in the IGO literature. Legitimacy is granted by the citizens of member states that create IGOs, as well as by the states themselves. Intergovernmental organizations need this legitimacy to take the lead in solving pressing societal issues. As Buchanan and Keohane (2006, p. 407) have noted, "the perception of legitimacy matters, because, in a democratic era, multilateral institutions will only thrive if they are viewed as legitimate by democratic publics." Cass (2005) has disentangled contemporary debates around the creation of the World Trade Organization (WTO); these debates focused on whether it was legitimate to create an organization with the power to decide issues of national economic interest from an international perspective. According to Cass, the WTO was ultimately successful because it emphasized the political aspect of an IGO, ensuring that all national realities were represented and considered within the organization; this stance eventually enabled the WTO to gain legitimacy among member states.

Although legitimacy is always judged by an actor or actors external to an organization, multiple characteristics determine whether an IGO is perceived as having a legitimate right to pursue its mission. For IGOs, legitimacy is anchored in both internal and external factors (Coicaud and Heiskanen 2001). Tallberg and Zurn (2019) have recently identified two main sets of factors that influence IGO legitimacy. The first factors are internal to the organization; they include institutional matters that the audience cares about, which can hinder or boost perceptions of legitimacy for a particular organization. For example, the degree of autonomy shown by the IGO's supranational bureaucracy (a secretariat or commission) is the key to ensuring legitimacy. The more independent the secretariat or commission, the stronger the perception of IGO legitimacy. Other researchers argue that cues and heuristics related to the IGO are more important than institutional features. They note than an IGO can gain legitimacy as a consequence of national trust in politics. If the public in a particular society has a high level of trust in political institutions, they may extend that trust to international organizations and vice versa. In practice, most authors rely on the framework of bounded rationality to explain that these internal and external features are interrelated. While institutional factors are crucial, it is also important to consider how individuals and their societies form biased opinions about IGO legitimacy.

3.3.2 IGO Strategies

This subsection revisits some recent proposals (Federo and Saz-Carranza 2017) to introduce the study of strategic planning to IGOs. For this exercise, we have selected six approaches that public organizations typically use to design their strategic plans (see Bryson and Roering 1987) and applied them to IGOs. We also introduce and discuss instances when the IMO used strategic-planning approaches to create policies and treaties.

Stakeholder-Driven Strategies

When organizations have key interest groups (stakeholders) with different demands, they can be pulled in different directions, making it very difficult for managers to decide which direction to prioritize. In such cases, strategic negotiations can be fundamental to the survival of IGOs. Managers should consider strategic-negotiation approaches to bring stakeholders to the table to discuss possible strategies. According to Fisher and Ury (1981), it is important to distinguish the parties from the problem; most negotiations fail because parties treat the negotiation stage as an opportunity to defend their own positions. Instead, they should focus on jointly defining an issue, together with a set of possible scenarios that can resolve it. Through collective action, they should determine which set of actions will resolve the issue while providing maximum benefit to all of the involved parties. This approach may be of particular value in cases where some IGO member states have less influence than others, as it gives all members a voice during deliberations.

Realistically, jointly defining a problem will sometimes produce winners and losers around the negotiation table. However, members often find compromise positions that they can agree on. The key to implementing this strategic approach successfully lies in the ability to shift the mentality of all parties involved in negotiating the agreement. Members must accept that they are not negotiating to defend their own individual positions, but to solve a common problem. While it is legitimate for members to have particular interests when finding a solution, the final shared agreement should balance individual-member compromises for the good of the IGO.

Managers of IGOs planning to implement a stakeholder-based approach should begin by identifying all organizational stakeholders. At the most basic level, stakeholders are defined as individuals or organizations that affect (or are affected by) the actions of the organization in question (Freeman 1984). Managers should be as inclusive as possible at this stage of the process. It is better to begin with a longer list of stakeholders and have to remove a few than to discover that an important stakeholder has been overlooked, generating complaints about a particular policy.

The second stage involves classifying stakeholders. Mitchell, Agle, and Wood (1997) advise managers to determine the salience of stakeholders based on three attributes: urgency, power, and legitimacy. Urgency is the degree to which stakeholder claims demand an immediate response. Power is the degree to which stakeholders can force an organization to submit to their will, even when the organization does not want to. Legitimacy, in this context, reflects a moral status or stance that makes it possible to demand certain actions;

legitimacy is judged by organization users or society at large. Considering these three attributes, Mitchell, Agle, and Wood (1997) have proposed a system of classification, in which each stakeholder is defined through a combination of attributes. For example, a stakeholder who possesses great power, high levels of legitimacy, and a strong sense of urgency is categorized as a "definite stakeholder." Intergovernmental organization managers should prioritize definite stakeholders when developing their strategic plans. This classification system can help managers focus their actions and efforts towards stakeholders considered more salient to the organization.

In practice, IGOs must face another fundamental issue: assessing the degree to which stakeholder demands differ. As it is relatively common for IGO stakeholders to demand opposing actions, managers must engage in strategic negotiations to find compromise solutions. Organizational membership and control designs can determine which IGO stakeholders are the most influential. Intergovernmental organizations with restricted memberships experience less conflict because acceptance (as a member state) implies agreement to a common objective. For example, membership in NATO requires states to cooperate when any member experiences an armed attack; there is thus little conflict among member states. In IGOs with a more universal remit, such as the IMO or International Labor Organization (ILO), member states have a wide range of interests, which can stall the decision-making process. In such cases, IGO secretariats tend to be responsible for managing stakeholders; they develop the role of collecting and assessing stakeholder demands.

Results-Driven Strategies

It is worth noting that all IGOs are goal-directed entities, although the goals of individual IGOs can be more or less specific. We argue that IGO goals can serve as the glue that keeps varied members within the IGO. As a result, most IGOs have a strong focus on results. This focus translates into two different approaches when it comes to strategy: strategic-planning systems and logical incrementalism.

Lorange (1980) has pointed out that organizations need organizational frameworks that allow them to understand the goals and objectives they have to achieve, as well as how to invest their resources to achieve these desired goals and objectives. Such frameworks constitute strategic-planning systems. A good system enables a manager to capture all necessary information, from across the organizational hierarchy, in order to make the right decision. The idea underpinning this approach is that the whole organization needs to stand behind some grand objective that each developed organizational action contributes to accomplishing.

By contrast, logical incrementalism assumes that some of an organization's activities may not relate to an overarching goal. It recognizes that organizations often operate with multiple objectives that make sense for one department or unit, but not for another (Lindblom 1959; Quinn 1980). This separation results in multiple strategies; the role of managers is to coordinate strategies and ensure that they do not undermine or contradict each other. Lindblom (1959), who argued that small activities could ultimately achieve a larger objective, coined the term "incrementalism" to describe this approach. This framework is commonly used to understand how IGOs operate. The perspective has been widely adopted because most IGOs have general secretariats, which are then divided into several smaller departments with separate units for each country or area of action. Using this approach, an IGO can establish a general purpose, while allowing each unit or subsection to work toward its own goals and objectives, even if these vary significantly across units.

We argue that IGO managers should merge the two approaches when determining their organizational strategies. Developing a mid- or long-term strategy to achieve major goals seems fundamental to understanding the purpose of an organization. At the same time, the logical incremental approach provides separate divisions or units of the organization with adequate flexibility. Managers should work toward defining clear organizational goals or objectives, while allowing units or sections to have the flexibility their contexts require. Managers of IGOs must manage any tensions that arise as a consequence of allowing specific strategies to come into conflict with overall organizational goals and achievements.

According to Federo and Saz-Carranza (2017, p. 208), "strategic-planning systems can provide an overall framework for IGOs to follow, whereas logical incrementalism can supplement the system with appropriate smaller strategies that are easily modifiable for immediate needs." An interesting case, which illustrates how these two frameworks can be successfully combined, is the IMO. At its inception, the IMO's primary purpose was to promote and encourage maritime safety practices. Since then, it has expanded its mandate beyond maritime safety to include other issues, including efficient navigation, the prevention and control of pollution from ships, and the protection of the welfare of seafarers. The IMO is quite centralized in its organization-wide strategies. It has established a system through which member states institutionalize some overall organization-wide goals to pursue its mandates. In its 2016–2021 strategic plan, the IMO outlined numerous strategic directions related to organizational effectiveness, the development and maintenance of a comprehensive framework for shipping-related activities, and the promotion of environmental awareness among stakeholders.

Despite this general overarching strategy, the IMO has developed a logical incrementalist approach to orchestrating its operations. The IMO is structured with multiple committees (and subcommittees) capable of directing actions that target strategic goals, demonstrating its strong strategic-planning system. However, each committee is free to create its own micro-strategies to fulfil overall organization-wide goals, thus exemplifying logical incrementalism. For instance, the IMO Maritime Safety Committee holds regular meetings to discuss safety issues, such as reviewing proposals for a maritime cyber-security framework; this was a key agenda item at the committee's ninety-sixth session. The Maritime Environment Protection Committee convenes to develop marine pollution-related policies, establishing a Ballast Water Management System to prevent exposure to harmful aquatic organisms via the ballast water produced by ships. The formulation of such micro-strategies supports the established common framework within the IGO. The complex structure of the IMO demonstrates how an overarching strategic-planning system and a narrower logical incrementalist approach can complement each other, achieving intended organizational results both efficiently and effectively.

Environment-Driven Strategies

All organizations, regardless of size or operating sector, are influenced by their environments. In this context, the "organizational environment" includes other organizations and sector or country characteristics that influence the actions of organizations. When dealing with organizational environments, managers aim to reduce the uncertainty their organizations face. They consider external factors that could affect their organizations, occasionally predicting future shocks. In this way, the manager's role resembles that of a ship's lookout centuries ago. The lookout was permanently posted on the highest mast to watch the horizon for other ships, land, or possible hazards. In the same vein, managers act as lookouts for their organizations, making sense of the environment and anticipating possible hazards. Two key strategic-planning approaches underscore this environmental complexity: the concept of dynamic capabilities and the Miles and Snow framework.

Teece, Pisano, and Shuen have defined the concept of dynamic capabilities for business organizations as "the firm's ability to integrate, build, and reconfigure internal and external competences to address rapidly changing environments" (1997, p. 516). Initially, this concept described organizations operating in rapidly changing industries, such as those related to technology. In recent years, however, the concept has been used to understand organizations operating in sectors not generally associated with a highly turbulent organizational environment. Studies have argued that organizations must enhance their capabilities, including both internal resources and competencies, to prepare for changes in their environment. This has a strong impact on organizational processes, routines, and learning approaches, which must be modified to achieve the flexibility that organizations need to adapt to external change. Researchers have argued that, in rapidly changing environments, only organizations that react and adapt in time will survive (DiMaggio and Powell 1983). Most of the literature on dynamic capabilities relates to the manufacturing industry; for this reason, the main argument has focused on changing the processes used to develop new products or using old products in new ways (see, for example, Zahra and Nielsen 2002). For organizations that do not produce goods, adapting to change can involve decentralizing, building strategic alliances, or, in the case of international organizations, increasing local autonomy.

While the dynamic-capabilities concept focuses on changing organizations to face their environments, the Miles and Snow framework departs from the idea that a successful strategy consists of interactions between an organization and its environment. It views organizations as actors playing an active role in developing their environments. Just as environments can change organizations, so organizational actions can change environments (Miles and Snow 1978). In their seminal work, which analyzes strategy for public-sector organizations, Boyne and Walker (2004) argue that public managers typically use three strategies when considering the Miles and Snow framework. "Prospectors" set out to change their environments, while also taking advantage of opportunities that arise from engaging with external factors. They work toward engineering their organizations to respond effectively to environmental pressures. The second type, "defenders," believe in their strategies and see the environment as source of possible problems, preventing them from successfully achieving their objectives. They tend to focus on the efficiency of organizational processes and to rely heavily on rules. The final type, "reactors," do not consider the environment unless it affects them directly. As their strategies tend to be ad hoc, they run the risk of responding too late to specific threats.

Both of these strategic approaches can be useful for IGOs. However, organizational characteristics must be considered when applying either the dynamic-capabilities perspective or the Miles and Snow framework. Among many IGO specifications, flexibility and independence are key characteristics to consider. As discussed above, it is important for organizations to adapt to their environments. Managers must identify external hazards and opportunities, while leading their organizations toward developing the flexibility they need to respond rapidly to their environments.

To return to the ship metaphor, when the lookout identifies an imminent threat, the ship must change direction to avoid it. Although the management literature refers to flexibility using different nomenclatures, such as "fluid" or "agile" organizations, the meaning is the same: employees and managers need a flexible mindset to embrace change, as well as rules and procedures that that enable small or large changes to be made relatively quickly. Similarly, when an organization depends on several others to operate or make strategic decisions, its ability to react rapidly to the environment can be seriously diminished. Although IGOs have very little independence from other organizations and tend to react slowly to external inputs, managers should take advantage of the organizations they depend upon to map and make sense of their environments. In other words, managers should use their lookouts to their advantage.

As discussed in Federo and Saz-Carranza (2017), the IMO is a clear example of an organization that has used both strategic approaches to its advantage, particularly when creating the 1974 Safety of Life at Sea (SOLAS) Convention. This treaty emerged in response to the 1967 Torrey Canyon disaster, in which oil pollution caused an environmental catastrophe. The IMO, described as a "sleeping beauty" (Schemeil 2013), has a reactive strategic stance, rarely moving unless provoked by extreme pressure from stakeholders. In this case, the disaster led to immense stakeholder scrutiny, prompting the IMO to adopt new arrangements for handling oil pollution, which were not included in the previous SOLAS Convention of 1960. International treaties usually come into force when a minimum number of states explicitly accept membership as parties to the convention. In this case, to streamline the treaty, the IMO enforced a tacit agreement that allowed an amendment to be agreed for enforcement on a specified date, unless member states objected to the amendment. This event proved that the IMO was both flexible enough to adjust a routine or process and independent enough to impose a new process, allowing members to converge toward a common goal. Managers can adopt a strategy that exploits both the dynamic-capabilities approach and the Miles and Snow framework by carefully considering an IGO's flexibility and independence. The 1974 SOLAS Convention continues to be enforced, with subsequent amendments implemented effectively through the new process.

In sum, strategic planning approaches depend on the overall organizational design of the IGOs. The challenge is identifying the approach that would fit with the design. Which of these strategies is the best one for IGO managers? Our response to this question is as follows: All and, at the same time, none. "All" because strategic approaches can coexist and be applied simultaneously, providing managers with valuable information and the perspective they need to achieve their goals successfully. "None" because none of these strategic approaches can guarantee organizational success.

4 Governance of IGOs

This section explores how IGOs are governed, particularly focusing on the role of the board of directors that are vested with the authority to oversee the IGO executives. In the first part of the section, we explore how the IGO leaders are selected. In this Element, we refer to IGO chief executives collectively as the CEOs. In the latter part of the section, we examine how IGO boards govern their respective organizations.

4.1 CEO Selection in IGOs

If IGO executives are important and potentially fundamental to making IGOs work, then their selection is a relevant issue. As a general rule, CEO selection is an important aspect of organizational governance (Goel and Thakor 2008), as CEOs play a crucial role in influencing and driving the strategic direction of organizations (Hambrick and Mason 1984; Miller et al. 1982). In a for-profit organization, the board is generally given full responsibility for selecting and appointing the CEO (Boivie et al. 2016; Hermalin and Weisbach 2001; Rutherford and Lozano 2018; Sebora and Kesner 1996). However, boards are not always responsible for selecting CEOs. In IGOs, CEOs are either directly chosen by member-state governments as principals or appointed by boards. When it comes to CEO selection, IGO members thus face a unique governance choice between two diverging paths. As previously discussed in relation to leadership, agency problems frequently arise between principals (i.e., member states, comparable to corporate shareholders) and agents (i.e., the CEO-led secretariats, comparable to corporate top-management teams) (Hawkins et al. 2006). To mitigate the agency problem, principals face a governance choice: either to directly select the agent or to use the board as a governance mechanism to select the agent on their behalf (Federo and Saz-Carranza 2020; Haas 1990).

4.1.1 Selecting IGO Executives: Plenaries or Boards

Intergovernmental organization members may adopt one of two different rationales when deciding how to select a CEO. On the one hand, principals may choose to protect their own interests by selecting the agent themselves (prioritizing direct and individual control by each principal). On the other hand, principals may choose to delegate the governance function to the board, which often provides more efficient organizational decision-making (i.e., collaborative efficiency).

Selection of CEOs can be a question of who actually decides, triggering a clash between attempts to mitigate principal-principal conflict in the plenary and delegating governance functions to the board to achieve collaborative efficiency. Family-owned firms, venture capital-backed firms, joint ventures, public-private partnerships, meta-organizations, and IGOs often choose to keep responsibility and decision-making within plenary or shareholder meetings. Thus, principals face a crucial choice: whether to directly control the agent by choosing the CEO or to forego effective control and rely on the board for efficient collaborative CEO selection.

The organization literature generally views CEO selection as a board responsibility. The underlying economy-oriented tenets of agency theory suggest that boards are better positioned to minimize adverse selection (Fama and Jensen 1983; Jensen and Meckling 1976), particularly when it comes to hiring CEOs. Boards are better able to identify and assess the characteristics and qualifications of CEO candidates (Zajac 1990). For this reason, CEO selection is generally understood to be a board responsibility (Boivie et al. 2016) and a board's ultimate control function (Mizruchi 1983).

However, boards do not always choose CEOs. In IGOs, principals often replace boards in selecting CEOs. In fact, the founding documents of many IGOs explicitly state that the principals are responsible for CEO selection. The WTO, International Telecommunications Union (ITU), and International Organization for Migration (IOM) have constitutions that unequivocally state that principals directly elect CEOs. This observation deviates from the general assumption that boards have the exclusive responsibility of choosing CEOs to mitigate adverse selection. The fact that some IGO boards do not choose CEOs creates a theoretical gap in the literature on CEO selection. Surprisingly, this literature overlooks the possibility that principals could select CEOs. We therefore propose that the governance choice in CEO selection involves the question of who selects the CEO, as well as whether insider or outsider candidates are hired. This alternative view adds nuance to the tenets of agency theory on CEO selection, as the governance choice underlying CEO selection embodies the paradoxical rationales of agency control and collaborative efficiency.

On the one hand, we argue that agency control in CEO selection is about managing the diverging interests of principals during the CEO selection process. This is particularly evident in organizations with strong and influential owners, prone to generating principal-principal conflict among shareholders (e.g., Young et al. 2008). A certain level of distrust among the principals promotes self-preservation by ensuring individual control over key organizational decisions. This behavior can be manifested through CEO selection, in which principals are more likely to be incentivized to select a preferred agent directly.

On the other hand, we argue that collaborative efficiency in CEO selection is about whether several principals forego multiple agency relationships to ensure efficient decision-making (Allcock and Filatotchev 2010; Child and Rodrigues 2003). In contrast to agency control, collaborative efficiency rests on collectivist cooperation, based on a higher level of trust and a willingness to become vulnerable (Mayer et al. 1995). Principals may entrust an independent body to perform the governance function on their behalf. With this rationale, principals are more likely to delegate the CEO-selection function to the board, recognizing the board's known advantage in mitigating adverse selection.

To explore how and why IGOs appoint CEOs, data on all sixty-nine global IGOs during the first quarter of 2016 were hand-collected and a database of organizational characteristics was built, drawn from each IGO's official documents. These sources included statutes, constitutions, terms of reference, procedural rules for main bodies, financial regulations, and annual reports. Any missing data were gathered by contacting the IGO secretariat directly. Data provided by IGO officers were added to the database. In an extremely small number of cases, information gaps were filled using data drawn from IGO websites.

A categorical variable indicating whether CEO selection was carried out by principals or the board was coded. Out of sixty-nine cases, fourteen IGOs used their boards to select CEOs, while fifty-five IGOs used their principals. Although the distribution of binary values was not equally divided across cases (20 versus 80 percent), this was not a rare event (see Figure 5 for

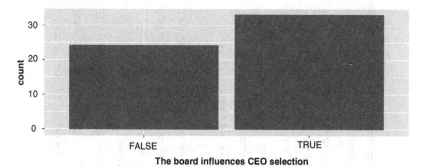

Figure 5 Distribution of the board responsible for the CEO-selection function
Source: Saz-Carranza, Fernandez-i-Marin, Federo, and Losada (2018).

Table 1 Hypotheses and findings

Hypothesis	Support	Coefficient	Prob. > 0	Prob. < 0	Who selects?
Membership structure					
Membership diversity					
(H1) Heterogeneity (Polity2)	Yes	−6.6800	0.0051	0.9949	Principals
Membership dispersion					
(H2) Number of members	Yes	0.5630	0.9985	0.0015	Board
Organizational characteristics					
Direct effect					
(H3) Organizational complexity: BI complex	Yes	4.5200	0.9990	0.0010	Board
(H4) Organizational size: Budget (log)	No –opposite	−0.9630	0.0061	0.9939	Principals
(H5) Organizational age	No	0.1970	0.8526	0.1474	Board
Interactions					
(H6a) BI complex * Heterogeneity (Polity2)	No	−2.8600	0.1435	0.8565	Principals
(H6a) BI complex * Number of members	No	−0.3810	0.0859	0.9141	Principals
(H6b) Budget (log) * Heterogeneity (Polity2)	No	0.3510	0.8536	0.1464	Board

(H6b) Budget (log) * Number of members	Yes – weak	0.1830	0.9978	0.0022	Board
(H6 c) Age * Heterogeneity (Polity2)	No	−0.1550	0.3670	0.6330	Principals
(H6 c) Age * Number of members	No	−0.0236	0.2640	0.7360	Principals

Source: Saz-Carranza et al. (2018).

descriptions of the cases). A logistic regression analysis on the binary variable (whether the plenary selects the CEO) against a vector of explanatory variables was subsequently run. Table 1 presents the summary findings.

4.1.2 The Role of Membership Structure in CEO Selection

Share-ownership is one driver of organizational self-identification that increases motivation and incentivizes involvement in oversight and strategic decision-making (Hambrick and Jackson 2000; Long 1980) among board directors (e.g., Adams and Ferreira 2008; Filatotchev and Bishop 2002) and firm employees (e.g., Hammer and Stern 1980; Pierce et al. 1991). Ownership structure is a strong determinant of governance design variation among different firms (La Porta et al. 1998; La Porta et al. 1999). Research has shown that diversity and concentration are two aspects of ownership structure that influence various strategic paths, including investment risk-taking and spending (e.g., Amihud et al. 1990; Baysinger et al. 1991; Haleblian et al. 2009), internationalization (e.g., Chen, 2008; George et al. 2005; Oesterle et al. 2013), and executive successions (e.g., Handler 1994; Kang and Shivdasani 1995). Following these studies, we have analyzed the way in which ownership structure influences CEO selection. In the context of IGOs, ownership structure pertains to the membership structure; we have therefore explored how membership diversity and concentration are associated with CEO selection in these organizations.

Membership Diversity

In accordance with agency theory, shareholders (as principals) are assumed to have generally homogenous preferences. However, principals often cluster into separate strategic groups with heterogenous preferences (Peng et al. 2004). These are more likely to be conflicting (Hoskisson et al. 2002), causing principal-principal conflict (Young et al. 2008). In the business literature, ownership diversity occurs when individual principals differ significantly in their characteristics and firm-investment intentions (Sur et al. 2013). Ownership diversity also reflects the extent to which shares are held by the state, foreign or local entities, individuals, family, business groups, funds, or other entities (Denis and McConnell 2003). It can influence the type of CEO selected, given that a dominant characteristic among owners suggests converging interests. For instance, firms with a higher percentage of insider-director ownership are likely to choose CEOs from their internal talent pools, suggesting a congregated interest among insiders (Boeker and Goodstein 1993). Owner diversity tends to reduce characteristic-based trust (Zucker 1986), incentivizing principals to protect their own preferences by taking individual control over various types of organizational decision-making, including CEO selection, which influence organizational direction. In firms with diverse ownership, uncertainty arising from the preferences of fellow principals tends to encourage active principal participation during CEO selection. In this study of IGOs, ownership diversity is associated with membership diversity (specifically differences between IGO member states).

To assess membership diversity, we measured the variable based on Marshall and Jaggers' (2002) polity index of level of democracy in states to calculate each IGO's internal standard deviation, based on its members. The "level of democracy" provides an indication of state preferences and behavior. Similar levels of democracy among states are assumed to signify homogenous preferences. The greater the IGO's standard deviation, in relation to its member states' level of democracy, the greater its heterogeneity and diverse preferences. Ownership diversity was found to have a high probability of strongly affecting the likelihood of principals themselves selecting the CEO (with a coefficient of -6.68 and a probability of 99.49 percent).

Membership Dispersion

The business literature argues that the distribution of firm ownership determines overall governance designs (Bebchuk and Roe 1999). Concentrated ownership suggests greater principal control (Demsetz and Lehn 1985), due to increased incentives to monitor and introduce changes into the organization (Bethel and Liebeskind 1993). By contrast, dispersed ownership implies reduced principal control and greater managerial power (Greckhamer 2016) because less shareholding leaves principals with minimal incentives and capacity to exert influence over management (Coffee 2001; Leech and Leahy 1991).

This Element argues that such assumptions also apply to CEO selection. In firms with concentrated ownership, greater risks are associated with larger investments, incentivizing principals to choose their preferred CEO to protect their own interests (Leech and Leahy 1991). Firms with dispersed ownership have more principals and are more likely to be professionally managed (Finkelstein and Hambrick 1989); principals are thus likely to cede control over key organizational decision-making. Group size is the classic driver of collective-action problems (Olson 1965). Although there is increased need for control, due to the aggravated agency problem of management self-interest dominating shareholder interests

(Daily et al. 2003), greater ownership dispersion can lead to freeriding among the principals monitoring agents (Gorton and Schmid 1999). As more principals lose incentives to monitor, delegating the governance function (including CEO selection) to the board can produce a more efficient decision-making mechanism. In this case, boards are more likely to select CEOs because they are able to balance the diverging interests of multiple principals, while choosing suitable candidates. This study thus conflates ownership dispersion with membership dispersion.

To assess membership dispersion, the variable was measured using IGO membership size, taken from IGO annual reports. More member states in an IGO suggests greater dispersion. The variable was logged and centered to the mean. Ownership dispersion was found to have a weaker but highly probable effect on the likelihood of CEO selection being delegated to the board (with a coefficient of 0.56 and a probability of 99.85 percent).

4.1.3 The Effect of Organizational Characteristics

Governance varies across organizations (Aguilera et al. 2008). Several organizational characteristics, including complexity, size, and age, are contextual conditions that typically influence CEO selection (e.g., Datta and Guthrie 1994; Guthrie and Datta 1998; Zhang and Rajagopalan 2010). Most previous studies have investigated how such organizational characteristics determine whether selected CEOs have specific qualities, such as experience, age, or insider/outsider status (e.g., Datta and Rajagopalan 1998; Ocasio and Kim 1999). By contrast, the current study analyzes how organizational complexity, size, and age influence the principals' decision to either select the CEO themselves or to delegate CEO selection to the board.

Organizational complexity refers to the amount of differentiation along various elements and processes that constitute the organization (Dooley 2002). It covers a wide range of organizational design structures and features, including the presence of multiple subunits, governance levels, and highly developed processes (Brickley et al. 1997). In this way, it imposes more information-processing tasks on the governing body (e.g., Bushman et al. 2004; Galbraith 1974; Henderson and Fredrickson 1996; Mintzberg 1973). Given the information asymmetry arising from the disconnect between shareholders and firm operations, principals typically have imperfect knowledge for making important decisions, such as selecting a suitable CEO to manage complex organizational settings. Boards therefore become a more efficient mechanism, carrying out governance functions on behalf of the principals. As they are closer to operations, boards are better placed to understand organizational processes and the organization's leadership requirements.

This study has measured organizational complexity using Boehmer, Gartzke, and Thompson's (2004) IGO codification, based on the following three-point scale of institutionalization: (1) Minimal organizations with small secretariats that focus on research, planning, and information gathering; (2) Structured organizations with bureaucracies that implement policies; (3) Interventionist organizations with mechanisms for mediation, arbitration and adjudication, and/or other means of coercing state decisions. Minimal IGOs were used as the reference category for low organizational complexity, and coded as 0. Categories 2 and 3 were collapsed to retain degrees of freedom (using "structured" and "interventionist" categories did not alter the results); high organizational complexity was coded as 1. Organizational complexity was found to strongly and clearly increase the likelihood of CEO selection being delegated to the board (with a coefficient of 4.52 and a probability of 99.9 percent).

Most studies assume that organization size is an important contingency variable in CEO selection (Guthrie and Datta 1998). Size is an indicator of tangible resources, suggesting larger pools of financial and managerial resources capable of preventing organizational failure (Mitchell 1994). The business literature suggests that large firms attract more qualified labor as well as capital (Bruderl and Shussler 1990). Like complexity, size determines how highly developed the organizational structures and processes become. Large firms generally find it more difficult to manage and coordinate internal activities (Chandler 1962). When it comes to CEO selection, the combination of more available labor and greater difficulty understanding firm operations exacerbates the risk of adverse selection, if a CEO is selected by principals with little knowledge of how the firm operates. In large firms, principals may have few opportunities to become good evaluators, capable of matching the qualifications of CEO candidates with organizational needs. In large and complex organizations, the board is often the most efficient structure for selecting CEOs, given its proximity to day-to-day activities (Zahra and Pearce 1989).

Organizational size is measured via annual operational expenditures, including projects and administrative expenses disclosed in IGO annual financial reports. In the case of international financial institutions (IFIs), we have excluded capital expenditures, which do not constitute part of the annual budget and are considered extraordinary events. The variable was also logged and centered to the mean. Organizational size is found to increase the likelihood of principals selecting the CEO (with a coefficient of -0.96 and a probability of 99.39 percent).

When it comes to organizational age, researchers claim that older organizations are more formalized in their functioning (Pugh et al. 1968). Older organizations have generally developed widely accepted and institutionalized routines and cultures, which are already embedded into organizational systems

(Cyert and March 1963). According to Guthrie and Datta (1998), organizational age is correlated with the likelihood that candidates with longer tenure and experience within the organization will be elected as CEOs, based on their knowledge of the organization. Age also increases process-based trust within organizations (Kale et al. 2002). As time goes by, organizational actors build mutual experience, forging trust in the process (Stuart and Podolny 1996; Zucker 1986). As more trust emerges over time, the extent to which principals directly control agents becomes less relevant (Gulati and Westphal 1999). Given that CEO selection is an organizational function that is likely to develop over time, we hypothesize that principals are more willing to delegate this function to the board in organizations that already have an established process.

The age of IGOs was computed using IGO founding dates. The number of years was logged and centered on its mean. Age was found to have a weak effect on CEO selection; this relationship has low probability (with a coefficient of 0.20 and a probability of 85.26 percent).

Studies have explored the level of technological intensity and environmental dynamism, which are thought to determine organizational structures (Mintzberg 1993). We therefore examined whether a particular industry characteristic (whether the IGO belonged to the financial sector, as the IFI does) had an effect on CEO selection. Compared to other industries, the financial industry entails greater informational asymmetries and a more significant moral hazard risk, which a board could address. It is worth noting that financial-sector IGOs were associated with the likelihood that CEO selection would be delegated to the board (with a coefficient of 3.58 and a probability of 98.76 percent).

Durand and Vargas (2003) have argued that organizational complexity can moderate the effect of ownership structure on organizational performance. Although they found no support for this thesis, while Greenwood, Deephouse, and Li (2007) found no support for the direct or indirect effects of organizational complexity on organizational performance, we nevertheless argue that these relationships may be important, in relation to CEO selection. They are certainly worthy of further testing. Organizational complexity exacerbates information asymmetry, heightens managerial opportunism, and increases monitoring costs, particularly in organizations with diverse and dispersed ownership structures (Durand and Vargas 2003).

Moreover, although organizational complexity and size are typically correlated because they both indicate organizational breadth and development (Bushman et al. 2004), it is important to account for them separately. A larger organization is not necessarily complex, and vice versa (Hall et al. 1967). As in the case of organizational complexity and size, organizational age is an indicator of the level of bureaucratization, which can facilitate or restrict certain organizational processes (Pierce and Delbecq 1977). The effect of membership structure on the choice to have principals or the board select the CEO is likely to be influenced by such organizational characteristics. Given their extensive bureaucratization, more complex, larger, and older organizations are likely to intensify the relationship between ownership structures and CEO selection.

Among moderating effects, only organizational size was found to have a high probability of reducing the effect of membership dispersion on CEO selection (with a probability of 99.78 percent); there was modest evidence (with 85.36 percent probability) that it also reduced the effect of membership diversity. Despite the lack of evidence, both organizational complexity and age were associated with reductions in the effect of membership structures on CEO selection. Overall, we infer that organizational characteristics have a negative moderating effect on the relationship between membership structures and CEO selection.

4.1.4 Lessons from CEO Selection

In CEO selection, the main objective of this section has been to identify factors that influence the governance choice underlying CEO selection, in which the principals must choose between selecting the CEO themselves or delegating the CEO-selection function to the board. Our findings suggest that membership structure clearly influences this governance choice. On the one hand, membership diversity is associated with principals taking charge of CEO selection. This finding is consistent with prior research, which suggests that different ownership types increase uncertainty because different strategic groups within organizations have siloed interests (e.g., Peng et al. 2004). Principals are more likely to pursue individual control to protect their own interests and to reduce opportunistic behavior among fellow principals (e.g., Chen et al. 2014).

On the other hand, membership dispersion is associated with board responsibility for the CEO-selection function. This parallels the long-standing agency-theory assumption that the board becomes an efficient governance mechanism in manager-controlled firms with diffused ownership (Jensen and Meckling 1976). This study contributes to the literature on CEO selection by helping to understand the board's important responsibility for appointing CEOs. Instead of tapping into the debate about whether boards should choose insider or outsider candidates for the post, we offer an alternative insight into principals themselves choosing the CEO.

Selection of CEO transcends the typical principal-agent assumption that this function is delegated to boards to mitigate adverse selection. In fact, CEO selection can also be a challenge to address principal interests. This study ultimately explores the principal-principal conflict that can arise during CEO selection (Young et al. 2008), with strong implications for organizational types that are prone to such challenges. For instance, family firms (e.g., Aguilera and Crespi-Cladera 2012), joint ventures (e.g., Filatotchev and Wright 2011), venture-capitalist-backed firms (e.g., Bruton et al. 2010), professional service partnership firms (e.g., Greenwood and Empson 2003), public-private partnerships (e.g., Phan et al. 2005), trade associations (e.g., Mohr and Spekman 1994), and meta-organizations (e.g., Gulati et al. 2012) may struggle to select CEOs because their principals have competing interests. Delegating governance functions to the board may not be the most suitable choice, particularly when there is high relational uncertainty among principals (e.g., Das and Teng 1996). Thus, the implication for management and governance is that dispersed principals or principals with antagonistic principal-principal relations will delegate to their boards the task of selecting the CEO.

This research demonstrates the influence of different organizational characteristics on CEO selection. Our findings show that only organizational complexity and size have a high probability of affecting the selection decision (e.g., Zhang and Rajagopalan 2010). While the effect of complexity is expected to transfer CEO selection to the board, the effect of size increasing principal control suggests that principals tend to reduce risks as they accumulate increased investments. As this study has used IGO budgets to measure organization size, and IGO budgets are largely based on principals' contributions, the likelihood that principals will ensure effective control to protect their own interests becomes a greater concern. The implication of this finding is that we may expect boards to select CEOs in complex organizations, while principals (i.e., members) will keep CEO selection responsibilities in large organizations.

As for the modest probability effect of age, the development of organizational processes over time may be less evident in IGOs than in other types of organizations. The legalistic and political nature of IGOs prevents them from making abrupt changes to organizational processes agreed among member states at the time of inception. Decision-making in these organizations requires the explicit consent of principals. For this reason, IGOs typically have strong inertial forces when it comes to changing the way they operate. Trust building may not occur among principals, who are often government representatives with high turnover frequency, as national governments change via domestic electoral cycles. Intergovernmental organizations may not evolve organically; they lack the dynamic nature of firms and other nonprofit entities, which can easily adapt and adjust to environmental needs.

Furthermore, very few organizational variables have relevant moderating effects on the relationship between membership structure and CEO selection. Our findings mirror previous studies, which found no moderating effects of complexity (e.g., Durand and Vargas 2003; Greenwood et al. 2007) or size on the effect of membership structures. Of more interest is the common thread linking organizational variables. Our study provides definite, if weak, evidence of the negative moderating effects of organizational characteristics on the influence of membership structure on CEO selection. These findings deviate from our own expectation that organizational variables should intensify such influence. Instead, these organizational characteristics reduce the effect of membership structures. This finding is in line with the barriers view of Boivie et al. (2016) in relation to organizational characteristics, whereby organizational complexity and size exacerbate information-processing needs. We provide evidence that organization-level factors are more likely to aggravate structural inertia, which may influence the governance choice on CEO selection.

It is also worth noting the effect of the variable indicating whether an IGO belongs to the financial sector. This variable suggests that financial IGOs are more likely to delegate CEO selection to their boards. This result echoes previous studies, which have suggested that financial institutions are subject to greater informational asymmetries, moral hazard risk, and higher levels of government regulation (Levine 2004) than other firms (Furfine 2001; Macey and O'Hara 2003). In this context, the board becomes a neutral, competent body that can mitigate adverse selection while effectively selecting a CEO and addressing principal interests. Despite somewhat weak evidence, our findings show that rotational board membership is associated with boards responsible for the CEO-selection function. This finding follows the notion that principals given equal opportunities to join the board and influence decision-making are more willing to forego immediate control.

4.2 Overseeing IGO Strategy Making

This subsection argues that the boards of directors should be responsible for monitoring strategy making in IGOs by overseeing the design, implementation, and evaluation of organizational strategies.

4.2.1 The Role of Boards in IGO Strategy Making

Intergovernmental organization managers do not work alone to develop strategic plans; they generally collaborate with a board of directors. However, the boards of directors have varying levels of involvement in developing organizational strategies. Some boards adopt a hands-off approach and focus on monitoring the development and implementation of the strategy. Others merely hold the manager accountable for organizational outcomes. However, some boards do participate actively in the strategy-making process. They do this by collaborating with the manager; the final strategy emerges as a team effort. Board involvement and its impact on organizations has been a topic of interest among corporate-governance scholars (see, for example, Nicholson and Kiel 2007; Van den Berghe and Levrau 2004; Zahra and Pearce 1990).

However, little is known about the extent to which IGO boards engage with managers to successfully achieve strategy-making objectives. In 2017, the WB released a statement announcing that its president and executive directors were working together to develop new operational strategies to address the deprivation crisis in sub-Saharan Africa and Yemen. A similar announcement in 2010 reported that the IMF Director General and Executive Board had extensively discussed and deliberated various strategies for providing exceptional debt relief to poor countries hit by catastrophic natural disasters.

Even though the vast majority of IGOs are governed by boards of directors, most of which have mandates explicitly stating that they must engage actively in the strategy-formulation process, many IGO boards do not participate actively in that process. It is therefore essential to delve into their role when developing an organizational strategy. This section addresses the degree of involvement that IGO boards ought to have in the strategy-making process. It also identifies governance designs associated with optimal levels of board involvement.

The following section builds on empirical evidence collected during previous research, published by Federo and Saz-Carranza (2018). Sixteen IGO boards were analyzed to collect empirical evidence. It is challenging to fully understand levels of board involvement, requiring both a descriptive approach and also a fine understanding of how different actors perceive their own levels of involvement in strategic decision-making. An inductive fuzzy-set qualitative comparative analysis was used to examine the sixteen boards. It identified various levels of board involvement, associated with highly effective and less effective strategy formulation.

The sixteen cases were based on IGOs analyzed by the Multilateral Organization Performance Assessment Network (MOPAN) between 2011 and 2014. The following organizations have been included in this study: the International Fund for Agricultural Development (IFAD), Joint United Nations Program on HIV/AIDS (UNAIDS), United Nations Development Program (UNDP), United Nations Environment Program (UNEP), United Nations Population Fund (UNPF), United Nations High Commissioner for Refugees (UNHCR), United Nations Children's Fund (UNICEF), United Nations Relief and Works Agency for Palestinian Refugees in the Near East (UNRWA), United Nations Entity for Gender Equality and the Empowerment of Women (UNWomen), World Food Program (WFP), WHO, WB, Asian

Development Bank (ADB), African Development Bank (AfDB), and Inter-American Development Bank (IDB). All of these IGOs are large, with annual budgets over €100 million.

To assess the performance of these IGOs, we have focused on how effective they are at formulating strategies as an outcome of interest. To operationalize this approach, we have followed McNulty and Pettigrew (1999), distinguishing between strategy quality and the quality and use of performance-evaluation information. The MOPAN valuation of IGO strategy quality is based on four criteria: (1) whether the strategy is focused on results; (2) whether organization-wide strategies are based on mandates; (3) whether strategies focus on cross-cutting priorities identified by the mandate; and (4) the extent to which country strategies focus on results. To assess the quality and use of performance information, MOPAN focuses on the extent to which evaluations comply with control procedures and existing quality standards, and whether they are used in organizational planning.

This Element views board features as the conditions in which strategies are formulated. A group of experienced coders reviewed the MOPAN reports, alongside internal documents from each organization, to assess the frequency of board meetings, the existence of executive committees, the presence of full-time directors, the number of committees they participated in, and whether boards were involved in CEO selection (see Federo and Saz-Carranza 2018 for full methodological details).

Although the analysis found that no single board feature was sufficient to yield the required outcome, various board configurations were associated with the development of effective strategies. Table 2 shows the range of configurations of board involvement in IGOs, also known as "solutions." It distinguishes IGOs that are highly effective in strategy formulation from those that are less effective. In particular, two board dynamic configurations are associated with better strategy formulation, although they differ in line with IGO complexity.

The first configuration is particularly well-suited to highly complex IGOs; it is characterized by full-time directors and very frequent board meetings. The directors and board members participate in many board committees and are involved in CEO selection. Intergovernmental organizations with this configuration include the WB, ADB, and IDB. This finding suggests that increased board–director interaction complements the increased use of director resources to facilitate better information processing in highly complex organizations.

The second configuration is applicable to organizations that are less complex, in which a different board dynamic configuration is associated with successful strategy formulation. This configuration features low-frequency board meetings, no executive committee, and a board that is not involved in CEO selection.

Table 2 Configurations of board involvement in IGOs

Configurations	Highly effective strategy-formulation solutions		Less effective strategy-formulation solutions		
	1	2	3	4	5
Board dynamics					
(1) High frequency of board meetings	●	⊗	⊗	●	⊗
(2) Existence of an executive committee		⊗	●	⊗	●
(3) Presence of full-time directors	●	⊗	⊗	⊗	⊗
Use of director resources					
(4) Participation in many committees	●	⊗	⊗	⊗	●
(5) Involved in CEO selection	●	⊗	⊗	⊗	●
Context					
*Organizational complexity	High	Low	Low	Low	Low
Consistency	0.91	0.92	0.82	1.00	0.90
Raw coverage	0.30	0.35	0.43	0.19	0.12
Unique coverage	0.30	0.35	0.43	0.19	0.12
Solution consistency	0.92		0.88		
Solution coverage	0.65		0.74		
Cases**	ADB IDB WB	UNEP UNICEF IFAD	UNHCR UNAIDS UNRWA	UNDP UNFPA	WHO

Notes:

(a) ● = present (core); • = present (peripheral)

(b) ⊗ = absent (core); ⊗ = absent (peripheral)

(c) A blank space is a "don't care" condition, which may be present or absent in a configuration.

* Organizational complexity refers to the context, which is the third dimension of our board involvement framework. Its inclusion in or absence from the solution does not change the solution's consistency or coverage metrics.

Source: Federo and Saz-Carranza (2018).

Intergovernmental organizations with this configuration include the UNEP, UNICEF, and IFAD. When considering less complex IGOs, our findings suggest that low levels of board interaction complement a reduced use of director resources, yielding highly effective strategy formulation. The boards of such organizations should focus on evaluating and approving proposals for their CEOs.

In a nutshell, our findings suggest that the optimal level of board involvement in strategy formulation depends on an organization's complexity, a factor that also determines its information-processing needs. When implementing a strategy in an IGO, the board should be aware that less complex organizations do better when their boards are less involved in strategy formulation, and vice versa.

4.2.2 Designing Boards to Monitor IGOs Effectively

While the previous section has argued that the degree of board involvement is key to formulating an IGO strategy, this section delves deeper into different board designs that make it possible to monitor how IGOs perform in implementing their strategies. It does this by analyzing governance mechanisms that enable IGOs to fulfil their mandates and stakeholder expectations. As discussed in Federo and Saz-Carranza (2020), the United Nations (UN) is a perfect case to study the mechanisms used by boards to monitor IGO performance. At present, thirty-four IGOs have been established or incorporated under the UN system to pursue different mandates. These IGOs govern and shape the institutional environments in which firms, national governments, public entities, and nonprofit organizations operate (e.g., Bach and Newman 2014; Shaffer 2015). However, many UN-system IGOs barely meet or fail to meet minimum performance thresholds (Federo and Saz-Carranza 2017). Why do so many IGOs underperform? Although the literature offers several explanations, the main reason seems to be that top managers at the national level often omit the mandates that their IGO secretariats have developed. As in a classic principal-agent relationship, IGOs must be able to closely monitor the behavior of member states to ensure that they act in line with IGO mandates.

Federo and Saz-Carranza (2020) have applied a configurational approach to reveal a board-design typology associated with highly effective monitoring of UN-system IGOs. The analysis uses data from thirteen global IGOs under the UN system, assessed by MOPAN. The structural features analyzed in the study are board size (operationalized in absolute and relative terms), number of board committees, presence of an executive committee, and presence of a board secretary. Other board features that potentially affect board monitoring are excluded because they are not relevant in the configurations (i.e., board independence, voting rights, and director busyness). The analysis was carried out using a fuzzy set qualitative comparative analysis (QCA) to identify the configurations. This allowed for the identification of four board

Organizational complexity

		Low	High
Distribution problem	**Low**	A-I. Less Complex IGO with low-level distribution problem (e.g, UNICEF) *Reinforced Board*	A-III. Complex IGO with low-level distribution problem (e.g, IFAD) *Symbolic Board*
		absolute board size — Large; relative board size — Low; number of committees — Low; executive committee — No; board secretary — Yes	absolute board size — Small; relative board size — Low; number of committees — Low; executive committee — No; board secretary — No
	High	A-II. Less Complex IGO with high-level distribution problem (e.g, UNEP) *Egalitarian Board*	A-IV. Complex IGO with high-level distribution problem (e.g, WB) *Bureaucratic Board*
		absolute board size — Large; relative board size — High; number of committees — Low; executive committee — No; board secretary — No	absolute board size — Large; relative board size — Low; number of committees — High; executive committee — Yes; board secretary — No

Figure 6 Typology of IGO board designs

Source: Federo and Saz-Carranza (2020).

designs – presented in Figure 6 – which reflect the interplay between two governance constraints arising from IGO characteristics: the level of organizational complexity and the extent of the distribution problem. These two IGO characteristics emerged from case knowledge, which is important for contextualizing the analysis and identifying any latent attributes that may explain the findings further (e.g., Parente and Federo 2019). Organizational complexity in IGOs refers to the diversity of mandates driving information asymmetry, whereas the distribution problem arises from the differing preferences of IGO member states when they act as multiple principals (Koremenos ct al. 2001).

The first archetype of board design refers to cases in which the level of organizational complexity is low, with a low-level distribution problem. One example is UNICEF, which has a *reinforced board* design that fits its low complexity and low-level distribution problem. It has a large pool of directors selected for their expertise and regional experience. Yet, despite the large board size, the number of UNICEF directors is relatively low, in comparison to total membership. There is a significant reduction in member-state representation on the board, which fits with the organization's low-level distribution problem.

The second archetype encompass cases in which organizational complexity remains low, with a high-level distribution problem. An example of this type of board configuration is the UNEP, which has an *egalitarian board*, enabling a voting scheme in which every state has one vote when directors are appointed. This example of a less complex IGO with a high-level distribution problem suggests that egalitarian boards are more focused on representation than efficiency, and thus cannot be highly effective in monitoring.

The third archetype is exemplified by complex IGOs with low-level distribution problems. The IFAD is a good example of this archetype, with a board design that focuses on efficiency; it has a small number of directors and just two highly specialized committees (audit and evaluation) established precisely to monitor the organization and eliminate redundant work by avoiding the need for a board secretary. We call this a *symbolic board*, as it is relatively small, given the size of the organization. Such boards must prioritize efficiency over representation to monitor effectively.

The fourth and final archetype described in the study relates to complex IGOs with high-level distribution problems. Of the thirteen IGOs analyzed, the WB perfectly fits this fourth archetype. The WB board structure is highly bureaucratic, with a large board and several specialized committees that provide skills, knowledge, and expertise. An executive committee oversees the performance of all committees and administrative policies adopted by the board. As the executive committee is sufficient to assist the board, no board secretary is needed. The WB is a complex IGO with a high-level distribution problem; its *bureaucratic board*, which emphasizes both efficiency and representation, is highly effective in monitoring.

The configurational approach provides a nuanced understanding of board designs by showing how board features strengthen each other; it also determines whether boards lean toward efficiency or representation logic. For example, large boards typically require support mechanisms, such as executive committees or board secretaries, to overcome coordination problems (see the examples of reinforced and bureaucratic boards). However, a large board without support mechanisms can be highly effective if it achieves efficiency by being well represented (see the example of an egalitarian board). Overall, our findings are in line with existing arguments about the importance of conjunctural causation, equifinality, and asymmetry in relation to board designs (e.g., Boivie et al. 2016; Misangyi et al. 2017).

While this research shows that multiple board structures can be effective, it also shows that effectiveness is contingent on IGO complexity and organizational distribution problems. The implication for IGOs – and member-based organizations at large – is that when designing boards to monitor IGO activities effectively, we must consider both organizational complexity and distribution problems, adapting the board structure accordingly.

5 Conclusions and Implications

The interconnected nature of the global landscape shines a spotlight on the important role played by IGOs in society today. Although IGOs have become arenas and instruments for facilitating cooperation among different transnational actors to solve global problems, many IGOs continue to fall short of expected results and are perceived as failed collective international undertakings. Although there is substantial research on IGO roles and the cooperation dilemma faced by state governments participating in IGOs, we still do not fully understand how these organizations actually function or operate. This lack of knowledge has inspired us to share insights about IGO strategy making, top executive leadership, and boards of directors to help researchers and practitioners understand how IGOs are managed and governed.

To understand the management and governance of IGOs, we have integrated a range of social-science disciplines, including international relations, management, public administration, and corporate governance. Our approach highlights several lessons, which enhance our understanding of these organizations and can help them improve organizational performance.

In relation to strategy-making, we argue that IGOs can choose from several available strategic-planning approaches to implement specific types of strategies. These approaches depend on core aspects of the strategic-planning process and the IGOs' organizational design features. Intergovernmental organizations that require consensus decision-making and have more stakeholders to consider should design stakeholder-driven strategies by combining strategic negotiations with stakeholder-based approaches. By contrast, IGOs with specific and divisible scope and a centralized structure should design results-driven strategies by combining logical incrementalism with strategic-planning systems. Intergovernmental organizations with high flexibility and independence are better off designing environment-driven strategies through a combination of the dynamic-capabilities approach and the Miles and Snow framework.

Although chief executives are responsible for strategy making, in some cases boards must facilitate the strategy-making process in order to produce better strategic plans. We argue that more complex IGOs need boards that are more involved in strategy making, while less complex IGOs may not require board participation.

Beyond strategy making, IGO boards can be designed to act as good general monitors of organizational activities. The design of IGO boards can help them oversee both strategy making and the subsequent implementation of strategies. We have built a typology of board designs, based on two underlying IGO organizational characteristics: levels of organizational complexity and distribution problems. For IGOs with low organizational complexity and low-level distribution problems, the board merely needs reinforcing to become a better monitor. By contrast, IGOs with high organizational complexity and high-level distribution problems need bureaucratic boards. Symbolic boards are recommended for IGOs with high organizational complexity and low-level distribution problems; egalitarian boards are appropriate for IGOs with low organizational complexity but high-level distribution problems.

Overall, these lessons in strategy-making suggest that IGOs should abandon the one-size-fits-all approach to management and governance. There are multiple ways to design IGO governance to achieve similar levels of acceptable outcomes across varied organizations.

When it comes to IGO leadership, this study explores two important topics, shedding light on the inner workings at the apex of these organizations. First, we present various leadership practices adopted by two prominent IGOs: NATO and the EU-CFSP. Using a network perspective, we provide evidence that IGO leaders use four leadership practices within their organizations: vision framing and strategy development, communicating with members, facilitating unity, and mobilizing support. These findings deviate from the traditional agency view of IGO leadership, in which IGO executives merely serve at the discretion of member states (as principals). We contend that IGO leaders typically become important network actors, who help to manage network relationships, not only with members, but also with other organizational stakeholders.

Second, we explore a governance choice that relates to CEO selection. In this, we depart from previous research, which has focused on whether CEOs are insiders or outsiders. Instead, we examine who really chooses IGO CEOs, and particularly whether the decision is made by member states directly or channeled through the board. We show evidence that an IGO's membership structure influences this governance choice. Chief executive officers are more likely to be chosen by principals in IGOs with diverse memberships; conversely, CEOs are more likely to be chosen by boards in IGOs with dispersed memberships. Although there is no general effect of organizational characteristics, our findings show that boards are more likely to choose the CEO in complex IGOs.

In sum, these IGO-leadership lessons suggest that the upper echelons of IGOs have peculiarities that must be understood. Although IGOs are organizations per se, their unique features prevent us from assuming that their leadership practices are directly parallel to those of other types of organizations, such as firms, public organizations, or nonprofits. This topic therefore deserves to be studied.

As we close this Element, the next section concludes with theoretical implications to inform future academic research, and with managerial implications to help practitioners improve IGO outcomes.

5.1 Theoretical Implications

This Element proposes several future research avenues. First, future research should explore relational leadership theories to deepen our understanding of the behaviors of IGO chief executives. By applying different theoretical perspectives, we can understand why IGO chief executives make specific decisions and adopt particular management styles within their respective organizations. Do IGO leaders differ in their management approaches? One interesting future research path could explore, for example, how our findings on Javier Solana, the subject of a leadership case, compare to studies of executive leaders of IGOs working in different policy sectors, with different governance and executive structures (e.g., WTO and ITU). How specific are our findings to Javier Solana? Do they reflect his individual traits?

Second, research on IGO strategy making is still in its infancy. This Element is among the first to underscore the importance of IGO strategy-making. Although organizational strategy-making has two phases, formulation and implementation, we have focused on strategy formulation and only partially on implementation. To help leaders produce better strategic plans for IGOs, we have investigated how strategies can be formulated and overseen effectively. Future studies should ascertain how the strategies and corresponding strategic-planning approaches proposed here can be implemented effectively to ensure better performance. When such studies are available, the field will have a complete picture of how strategy works in these organizations.

Third, future studies should also delve into the various mechanisms that can be used to develop a strategic plan, and how they impact the performance of IGOs. Promising research questions could include the following: Do participatory approaches, which empower stakeholders in the strategy-formulation process, lead to better IGO outcomes? Do different types of stakeholders have more influence on various organizational decision-making processes? How do IGOs encourage stakeholders to participate in such activities?

Fourth, it would be interesting for future studies of CEO selection in IGOs to examine other behavioral and political factors that could affect this governance choice: Who selects the CEO? Do personal relationships, informal networks, or the power of principals influence CEO selection in IGOs? Although IGOs are not subject to national jurisdictions, other institutional frameworks may influence the IGO CEO-selection process. Do culture and affinity play a role? Do member states exhibit observable normative behaviors that can ultimately influence CEO selection?

Fifth, future research should explore how the governance choice underlying CEO selection in IGOs is associated with organizational outcomes. It would be interesting to know whether principal-appointed CEOs outperform board-appointed CEOs, or vice versa. Does this choice affect different outcomes differently (i.e., efficiency versus effectiveness)?

Sixth, in considering CEO selection as a governance choice, how do IGOs compare to other nonconventional firms, which also experience principal-principal problems? It would be interesting to understand how this governance choice relates to joint ventures, professional service partnerships, and firms that are heavily controlled by family members, founders, venture capitalists, or institutional shareholders.

Seventh, this Element highlights the roles and functions of IGO boards of directors. Despite the importance of boards in IGO governance, very few studies have asked whether board design affects organizational functioning. We urge future researchers to study other aspects of board governance in IGOs. For instance, it would be interesting to identify their decision-making processes and inner workings, structural characteristics, composition, and the impact of these on board effectiveness and organizational outcomes. Moreover, the member states that constitute as "owners" of these organizations may have different board governance strategies. Research argues that different owners have distinctive social contexts that affect how they exert influence on the board (Federo et al. 2020). Thus, it is a fruitful path to explore how the social context of different member states affect board governance in IGOs.

Lastly, this Element uses emerging research methods that researchers can apply in future studies. For instance, we have analyzed board designs using QCA. This research method is a widely accepted technique for empirically examining causal complexity; its use corresponds with the multilayered and multifaceted factors that characterize and affect IGOs (Federo 2020). Moreover, using QCA is known as a reliable tool in building better typologies (Fiss, 2011). With the difficulty in creating an overarching typology to distinguish IGOs, perhaps exploring the capability of this approach in building typologies can be a fruitful path for IGO research. In a similar vein, we have analyzed CEO selection using Bayesian statistics. This technique has allowed us to carry out a statistical analysis of a medium-sized sample of global IGOs, despite having no previous research on our hypotheses concerning IGOs (e.g., Fernandez-i-Marin 2016). Overall, these two research techniques have great potential for future IGO research.

5.2 Managerial Implications

This Element also presents several findings of interest to practitioners. We divide them into two themes: managing and governing IGOs.

5.2.1 Managing IGOs

When it comes to managing IGOs, the first lesson that practitioners should take away from this Element is that strategic plans are very important for the performance of IGOs. Our research shows that many IGOs continue to operate without them. According to a large body of literature in the field of strategic management, strategic plans are essential for various types of organizations, providing an overall direction and a concrete means of measuring performance. The strategic-planning process ultimately helps many different organizations improve their performance. We believe that IGOs would benefit from devising strategic plans. This implies that IGO managers should develop strategic plans to guide the decision-making processes of their respective organizations.

The second lesson to take away from this Element is that IGOs need to put a premium on managing their stakeholders. They should begin by identifying and mapping their stakeholders, and then classify them to determine how their needs and demands can best be met. Intergovernmental organizations engage with various interest groups, which generally have conflicting expectations of how the organization should operate and function. By balancing the varied needs of a wide array of stakeholders, IGO managers can mitigate potential threats to their effective functioning and survival. Therefore, it is essential for IGO executives to map their stakeholders and facilitate agreement among them.

The third lesson that practitioners should bear in mind is this: when creating a strategy, IGO managers should work toward defining a clear organizational goal, while simultaneously giving units and sections the flexibility they need to operate in their own contexts. Although most IGOs have overarching mandates, some establish rigid goals that are not practical for the organization as a whole. Often, this is because the units comprising the organization do not have equal capacities to pursue set goals. Without flexibility, some will ultimately fail to accomplish the IGO mandate effectively. Other IGOs establish vague goals to allow different units to maneuver. This approach can result in inefficiencies, with some units deviating from the IGO mandate. Thus, IGO managers must address a classic organizational trade-off, by finding a balance between clear-cut goals and flexibility among units; in this way, they can mitigate the trade-off between efficiency and effectiveness when setting goals.

A fourth lesson that can be derived from this Element is that IGO executives should view their member states as a network that must be brokered to allow for collective action and avoid divisions between participants. Central to such an endeavor is the need to gauge the preferences of different member states. Intergovernmental organization executives should develop a collective strategy that reflects minority interests, as well as those of the main powers. The aim must be to ensure an equitable representation of voices and interests during decision-making processes (e.g., Saz-Carranza et al. 2020), and particularly when setting strategies, policies, and frameworks that affect the entire organization. The ability to reach a compromise among participants can legitimize decisions, making each member more likely to accept the results of negotiations. This implies that IGO executives are in essence brokers in relation to IGO members.

More importantly, the fifth implication for practitioners is this: it is essential to ensure that executives use all available formal and informal channels to communicate with member states. In this way, they can frame a common strategy and keep exchanges within the organization flowing. When parties disagree, executives should allow dissatisfied members to voice their dissatisfaction in sensible ways. Researchers have long recognized the benefits of open communication within organizations, including the possibility of embracing dissent. An open system facilitates ideas and reduces the likelihood that deference will become normalized among members. Sharing multiple perspectives during deliberations will improve decision-making processes.

5.2.2 Governing IGOs

The overall takeaway from this Element on IGO governance is that boards are very important to these organizations. Practitioners should consider two key lessons on board design. First, large executive boards typically require support mechanisms, such as executive committees or board secretaries, to overcome coordination problems among members. Although the logic of abilities posited by RDT suggests that larger boards attract resources that benefit the organization, being large is not always better. One counterargument is that larger boards give rise to inefficiencies. In particular, large boards mean more decision makers to potentially hinder decision-making processes or reduce incentives to carry out various functions. This implies that practitioners should consider incorporating support mechanisms (such as committees) to mitigate the disadvantages associated with larger boards.

Second, many different board structures can be effective. However, these are contingent on characteristics that contribute to IGO heterogeneity. The intersection between IGO complexity and distribution problems gives rise to governance needs that call for different board structures. To structure boards able to monitor IGO activities effectively, managers must consider both an organization's complexity and its distribution problems (among members), adapting the board structure accordingly.

As CEO selection in IGOs is a governance issue, principals must choose whether to select the CEO themselves or to delegate the CEO selection process to the board. This governance choice exemplifies a clashing rationale between agency control, which assumes that principals will protect their own interests by choosing a candidate to lead the organization, and collaborative efficiency, which presupposes that the board is a more efficient mechanism for choosing the top executive. This choice will be influenced by the IGO membership structure (i.e., concentration and diversity). Organizational complexity seems to moderate the relationship. One important lesson that practitioners can extract from this insight is that leaders play a crucial role in IGOs. As top executives represent the organization, the principals are highly incentivized to state their views during the CEO selection process. The tension between control and efficiency creates a dilemma for member states, particularly when it comes to prioritizing self-interest or the pursuit of collective actions. Together with previous findings related to IGO members, this finding implies that membership (i.e., the IGO principals) is of crucial importance in designing governance structures and allocating governance responsibilities – setting IGOs apart from other conventional nonmembership-based organizations.

Overall, organizational complexity is an important consideration for IGO governance designs. It not only affects the way in which IGO boards should be structured and designed, but also whether they are given more responsibilities. We advise practitioners to carefully consider the complexity of their organizations; as this Element has shown, varying levels of IGO complexity are associated with different governance designs, which affect how these organizations perform.

5.3 Concluding Remarks

Intergovernmental organizations have become important players in the international arena, as societal problems have also become more global in nature. They play a crucial role in facilitating cooperation between member states and other international actors, including multinationals, nonprofit organizations, and the general public. The lack of understanding about the way in which

IGOs function and operate inspired us to write this Element, since IGOs comprise a set of different types of organizations that need to be understood. We offer these preliminary insights into the inner workings of IGOs to help researchers and practitioners understand various understudied and underexplored facets of these organizations.

Despite several calls for IGOs to be more transparent about their internal affairs, particularly decision-making processes and activities, IGOs remain disconnected from the general public. It is therefore unsurprising that many IGOs are perceived by some of their own stakeholders as underperforming. Some IGOs have even been criticized for being "useless" at resolving global issues. Many commentators, for instance, have condemned the WHO for its handling of the Covid-19 pandemic. In a similar vein, the IMF was blamed for the recent financial crisis. World leaders continue to chastise the UN and EU. Yet, most of the current challenges that we face demand intergovernmental cooperation. Intergovernmental organizations, we believe, play a fundamental role in tackling these challenges, as they allow governments to come together and implement joint policies.

The main purpose of this Element is to improve the performance of IGOs. It does so by unpacking the differences in management and governance structures among IGOs and how they function, which is primarily relying on the member states that established them. We hope that this Element will correct several public misconceptions about these organizations, while encouraging academics, policy makers, and practitioners to continue working to improve the management and governance of IGOs and ultimately their performance.

Bibliography

Ackoff, R. (1970). A concept of corporate planning. *Long Range Planning*, 3(1), 2–8.

Adams, R. and Ferreira, D. (2008). One share–one vote: The empirical evidence. *Review of Finance*, 12(1), 51–91.

Agranoff, R. (2007). *Managing Within Networks: Adding Value to Public Organizations*. Washington, DC: Georgetown University Press.

Agranoff, R. and McGuire, M. (2001). Big questions in public network management research. *Journal of Public Administration Research and Theory*, 11 (3), 295–326.

Aguilera, R. V. and Crespi-Cladera, R. (2012). Firm family firms: Current debates of corporate governance in family firms. *Journal of Family Business Strategy*, 3(2), 66–69.

Aguilera, R. V., Filatotchev, I., Gospel, H., and Jackson, G. (2008). An organizational approach to comparative corporate governance: Costs, contingencies, and complementarities. *Organization Science*, 19(3), 475–492.

Allcock, D. and Filatotchev, I. (2010). Executive incentive schemes in initial public offerings: The effects of multiple-agency conflicts and corporate governance. *Journal of Management*, 36(3), 663–686.

Amihud, Y., Lev, B., and Travlos, N. G. (1990). Corporate control and the choice of investment financing: The case of corporate acquisitions. *The Journal of Finance*, 45(2), 603–616.

Bach, D. and Newman, A. (2014). Domestic drivers of transgovernmental regulatory cooperation. *Regulation & Governance*, 8(4), 395–417.

Barnett, M. N. and Finnemore, M. (1999). The politics, power, and pathologies of international organizations. *International Organization*, 53(4), 699–732.

Barnett, M. N. and Finnemore, M. (2004). *Rules for the World: International Organizations in Global Politics*. Ithaca, NY: Cornell University Press.

Baysinger, B. D., Kosnik, R. D., and Turk, T. A. (1991). Effects of board and ownership structure on corporate R&D strategy. *Academy of Management Journal*, 34(1), 205–214.

Bebchuk, L. A. and Roe, M. J. (1999). A theory of path dependence in corporate ownership and governance. *Stanford Law Review*, 52: 127.

Berns, K. V. and Klarner, P. (2017). A review of the CEO succession literature and a future research program. *Academy of Management Perspectives*, 31(2), 83–108.

Bethel, J. E. and Liebeskind, J. (1993). The effects of ownership structure on corporate restructuring. *Strategic Management Journal*, 14(S1), 15–31.

Boehmer, C., Gartzke, E., and Nordstrom, T. (2004). Do intergovernmental organizations promote peace? *World Politics*, 57(1), 1–38.

Boeker, W. and Goodstein, J. (1993). Performance and successor choice: The moderating effects of governance and ownership. *Academy of Management Journal*, 36(1), 172–186.

Boivie, S., Bednar, M. K., Aguilera, R. V., and Andrus, J. L. (2016). Are boards designed to fail? The implausibility of effective board monitoring. *Academy of Management Annals*, 10(1), 319–407.

Boyne, G. and Walker, R. (2004). Strategy content and public service organizations. *Journal of Public Administration Research and Theory*, 14 (2), 231–252.

Boughton, M. J. M. (2001). *Silent Revolution: The International Monetary Fund, 1979–1989*. Washington, DC: International Monetary Fund.

Brickley, J. A., Smith Jr., C. W. , and Zimmerman, J. L. (1997). Management fads and organizational architecture. *Journal of Applied Corporate Finance*, 10(2), 24–39.

Bruderl, J. and Schussler, R. (1990). Organizational mortality: The liabilities of newness and adolescence. *Administrative Science Quarterly*, 35(3), 530–547.

Bruton, G. D., Filatotchev, I., Chahine, S., and Wright, M. (2010). Governance, ownership structure, and performance of IPO firms: The impact of different types of private equity investors and institutional environments. *Strategic Management Journal*, 31(5), 491–509.

Bryson, J. (2011). *Strategic Planning for Public and Nonprofit Organizations: A Guide to Strengthening and Sustaining Organizational Achievement*. San Francisco, CA: Jossey-Bass.

Bryson, J. and Roering, W. (1987). Applying private-sector strategic planning in the public sector. *Journal of American Planning Association*, 53(1), 9–22.

Buchanan, A. and Keohane, R. O. (2006). The legitimacy of global governance institutions. *Ethics & International Affairs*, 20(4), 405–437.

Busenbark, J. R., Krause, R., Boivie, S., and Graffin, S. D. (2016). Toward a configurational perspective on the CEO: A review and synthesis of the management literature. *Journal of Management*, 42(1), 234–268.

Bushman, R., Chen, Q., Engel, E., and Smith, A. (2004). Financial accounting information, organizational complexity and corporate governance systems. *Journal of Accounting and Economics*, 37(2), 167–201.

Cass, D. Z. (2005). *The Constitutionalization of the World Trade Organization: Legitimacy, Democracy, and Community in the International Trading System*. Oxford, UK: Oxford University Press.

Castanias, R. P. and Helfat, C. E. (2001). The managerial rents model: Theory and empirical analysis. *Journal of Management*, 27(6), 661–678.

Chandler, A. D. (1962). *Strategy and Structure: History of the Industrial Enterprise*. Cambridge, MA: MIT Press.

Chen, S. F. S. (2008). The motives for international acquisitions: Capability procurements, strategic considerations, and the role of ownership structures. *Journal of International Business Studies*, 39(3), 454–471.

Chen, V. Z., Li, J., Shapiro, D. M., and Zhang, X. (2014). Ownership structure and innovation: An emerging market perspective. *Asia Pacific Journal of Management*, 31(1), 1–24.

Child, J. and Rodrigues, S. B. (2003). Corporate governance and new organizational forms: Issues of double and multiple agency. *Journal of Management and Governance*, 7(4), 337–360.

Chung, K. H., Rogers, R. C., Lubatkin, M., and Owers, J. E. (1987). Do insiders make better CEOs than outsiders? *Academy of Management Perspectives*, 1(4), 325–331.

Chwieroth, J. M. (2012). "The silent revolution": How the staff exercise informal governance over IMF lending. *The Review of International Organizations*, 8(2), 265–290.

Coffee Jr., J. C. (2001). The rise of dispersed ownership: The roles of law and the state in the separation of ownership and control. *Yale Law Journal*, 111(1), 1–82.

Coicaud, J. M. and Heiskanen, V. A. (2001). *The Legitimacy of International Organizations*. United Nations University Press: Tokyo, Japan.

Cyert, R. M. and March, J. G. (1963). *A Behavioral Theory of the Firm*. Englewood Cliffs, NJ: Prentice Hall, 169–187.

Daily, C. M., Dalton, D. R., and Rajagopalan, N. (2003). Governance through ownership: Centuries of practice, decades of research. *Academy of Management Journal*, 46(2), 151–158.

Das, T. K. and Teng, B. S. (1996). Risk types and inter-firm alliance structures. *Journal of Management Studies*, 33(6), 827–843.

Datta, D. K. and Guthrie, J. P. (1994). Executive succession: Organizational antecedents of CEO characteristics. *Strategic Management Journal*, 15(7), 569–577.

Datta, D. K., and Rajagopalan, N. (1998). Industry structure and CEO characteristics: An empirical study of succession events. *Strategic Management Journal*, 19(9), 833–852.

Demsetz, H. and Lehn, K. (1985). The structure of corporate ownership: Causes and consequences. *Journal of Political Economy*, 93(6), 1155–1177.

Denis, D. K. and McConnell, J. J. (2003). International corporate governance. *Journal of Financial and Quantitative Analysis*, 38(1), 1–36.

DiMaggio, P. and Powell, W. (1983). The iron cage revisited: Institutional isomorphism and collective rationality in organizational fields. *American Sociological Review*, 48(2), 147–160.

Dooley, K. (2002). Organizational complexity. *International Encyclopedia of Business and Management*, 6, 5013–5022.

Dror, Y. (1983). *Public Policy Making Reexamined*. New Brunswick, NJ: Transaction Publishers.

Durand, R. and Vargas, V. (2003). Ownership, organization, and private firms' efficient use of resources. *Strategic Management Journal*, 24(7), 667–675.

Eisenhardt, K. M. (1989). Agency theory: An assessment and review. *Academy of Management Review*, 14(1), 57–74.

Fama, E. F. and Jensen, M. C. (1983). Agency problems and residual claims. *The Journal of Law and Economics*, 26(2), 327–349.

Federo, R. (2017). Governing those who govern: Essays on the governance of intergovernmental organizations. Ph.D. dissertation, Universitat Ramon Lull.

Federo, R. (2020). Qualitative comparative analysis. In F. Badache, L. Kimber, and L. Maertens eds., *Introduction to International Organization Research Methods*. In press.

Federo, R., Ponomareva, Y., Aguilera, R. V., Saz-Carranza, A., and Losada, C. (2020). Bringing owners back on board: A review of the role of ownership type in board governance. *Corporate Governance: An International Review*. In press. doi: 10.1111/corg.12346.

Federo, R. and Saz-Carranza, A. (2015). A research approach to international governmental organizations: Examining executive boards and strategy. In J. Solana and A. Saz-Carranza, eds., *The Global Context: How Politics, Investment, and Institutions Impact European Businesses*. Barcelona: ESADEgeo, ESADE Business School, pp. 194–211.

Federo, R. and Saz Carranza, A. (2017). Devising strategic plans to improve organizational performance of intergovernmental organizations. *Global Policy*, 8(2), 202–212.

Federo, R. and Saz Carranza, A. (2018). A configurational analysis of board involvement in intergovernmental organizations. *Corporate Governance: An International Review*, 26(6), 414–428.

Federo, R. and Saz-Carranza, A. (2020). A typology of board design for highly effective monitoring in intergovernmental organizations under the United Nations system. *Regulation & Governance*, 14(2), 344–361.

Fernández-i-Marin, X. (2016). ggmcmc: Analysis of MCMC samples and Bayesian inference. *Journal of Statistical Software*, 70(9), 1–20.

Filatotchev, I. and Bishop, K. (2002). Board composition, share ownership, and "underpricing" of UK IPO firms. *Strategic Management Journal*, 23(10), 941–955.

Filatotchev, I. and Wright, M. (2011). Agency perspectives on corporate governance of multinational enterprises. *Journal of Management Studies*, 48(2), 471–486.

Finkelstein, S. and Hambrick, D. C. (1989). Chief executive compensation: A study of the intersection of markets and political processes. *Strategic Management Journal*, 10(2), 121–134.

Fisher, R. and Ury, W. (1981). *Getting to yes: Negotiating agreement without giving in*. New York, NY: Penguin Books.

Fiss, P. C. (2011). Building better causal theories: A fuzzy set approach to typologies in organization research. *Academy of Management Journal*, 54(2), 393–420.

Freeman, R. E. (1984). *Strategic Management: A Stakeholder Approach*. Boston, MA: Pitman.

French Jr., J. R. and Raven, B. (1959). The bases of social power. In D. P. Cartwright, ed., *Studies in Social Power* (150–167). Michigan: University of Michigan.

Furfine, C. H. (2001). Banks as monitors of other banks: Evidence from the overnight federal funds market. *The Journal of Business*, 74(1), 33–57.

Galbraith, J. R. (1974). Organization design: An information processing view. *Interfaces*, 4(3), 28–36.

Gelman, A., Stern, H. S., Carlin, J. B., Dunson, D. B., Vehtari, A., and Rubin, D. B. (2013). *Bayesian Data Analysis*. Boca Raton, FL: CRC Press, Chapman and Hall.

George, B., Walker, R. M., and Monster, J. (2019). Does strategic planning improve organizational performance? A meta-analysis. *Public Administration Review*, 79(6), 810–819.

George, G., Wiklund, J., and Zahra, S. A. (2005). Ownership and the internationalization of small firms. *Journal of Management*, 31(2), 210–233.

Geweke, J. (1992). Evaluating the accuracy of sampling-based approaches to the calculations of posterior moments. *Bayesian Statistics*, 4: 641–649.

Giambatista, R. C., Rowe, W. G., and Riaz, S. (2005). Nothing succeeds like succession: A critical review of leader succession literature since 1994. *The Leadership Quarterly*, 16(6), 963–991.

Gill, J. (2002). *Bayesian Methods: A Social and Behavioral Sciences Approach*. Boca Raton, FL: CRC Press, Chapman and Hall.

Goel, A. M. and Thakor, A. V. (2008). Overconfidence, CEO selection, and corporate governance. *The Journal of Finance*, 63(6), 2737–2784.

Gorton, G. and Schmid, F. (1999). Corporate governance, ownership dispersion and efficiency: Empirical evidence from Austrian cooperative banking. *Journal of Corporate Finance*, 5(2), 119–140.

Greckhamer, T. (2016). CEO compensation in relation to worker compensation across countries: The configurational impact of country-level institutions. *Strategic Management Journal*, 37(4), 793–815.

Greene, W. H. (2003). *Econometric Analysis*. Delhi: Pearson Education, India.

Greenhill, B., Ward, M. D., and Sacks, A. (2011). The separation plot: A new visual method for evaluating the fit of binary models. *American Journal of Political Science*, 55(4), 991–1002.

Greenwood, R., Deephouse, D. L., and Li, S. X. (2007). Ownership and performance of professional service firms. *Organization Studies*, 28(2), 219–238.

Greenwood, R. and Empson, L. (2003). The professional partnership: Relic or exemplary form of governance? *Organization Studies*, 24(6), 909–933.

Gulati, R., Puranam, P., and Tushman, M. (2012). Meta-organization design: Rethinking design in interorganizational and community contexts. *Strategic Management Journal*, 33(6), 571–586.

Gulati, R. and Westphal, J. D. (1999). Cooperative or controlling? The effects of CEO-board relations and the content of interlocks on the formation of joint ventures. *Administrative Science Quarterly*, 44(3), 473–506.

Guthrie, J. P. and Datta, D. K. (1998). Corporate strategy, executive selection, and firm performance. *Human Resource Management*, Published in cooperation with the School of Business Administration, The University of Michigan and in alliance with the Society of Human Resources Management, 37(2), 101–115.

Haas, E. B. (1990). *When Knowledge is Power: Three Models of Change in International Organizations* (Vol. 22). Oakland, CA: University of California Press.

Haleblian, J., Devers, C. E., McNamara, G., Carpenter, M. A., and Davison, R. B. (2009). Taking stock of what we know about mergers and acquisitions: A review and research agenda. *Journal of Management*, 35(3), 469–502.

Hall, R. H., Johnson, N. J., and Haas, J. E. (1967). Organizational size, complexity, and formalization. *American Sociological Review*, 32(6), 903–912.

Hambrick, D. C. and Jackson, E. M. (2000). Outside directors with a stake: The linchpin in improving governance. *California Management Review*, 42(4), 108–127.

Hambrick, D. C. and Mason, P. A. (1984). Upper echelons: The organization as a reflection of its top managers. *Academy of Management Review*, 9(2), 193–206.

Hammer, T. H. and Stern, R. N. (1980). Employee ownership: Implications for the organizational distribution of power. *Academy of Management Journal*, 23(1), 78–100.

Handler, W. C. (1994). Succession in family business: A review of the research. *Family Business Review*, 7(2), 133–157.

Harris, D. and Helfat, C. E. (1998). CEO duality, succession, capabilities and agency theory: Commentary and research agenda. *Strategic Management Journal*, 19(9), 901–904.

Hawkins, D. G. and Jacoby, W. (2006). How agents matter. In Hawkins, D. G., Lake, D. A., Nielson, D. L., and Tierney, M. J., eds., *Delegation and Agency in International Organizations*. Cambridge, UK: Cambridge University Press.

Hawkins, D. G., Lake, D. A., Nielson, D. L., and Tierney, M. J., eds. (2006). *Delegation and agency in international organizations*. Cambridge, UK: Cambridge University Press.

Henderson, A. D. and Fredrickson, J. W. (1996). Information-processing demands as a determinant of CEO compensation. *Academy of Management Journal*, 39(3), 575–606.

Hermalin, B. E. and Weisbach, M. S. (2001). Boards of directors as an endogenously determined institution: A survey of the economic literature (NBER Working Paper No. 8161). National Bureau of Economic Research.

Herrmann, P. and Datta, D. K. (2002). CEO successor characteristics and the choice of foreign market entry mode: An empirical study. *Journal of International Business Studies*, 33(3), 551–569.

Hillman, A. J. and Dalziel, T. (2003). Boards of directors and firm performance: Integrating agency and resource dependence perspectives. *Academy of Management Review*, 28(3), 383–396.

Hillman, A. J., Withers, M. C., and Collins, B. J. (2009). Resource dependence theory: A review. *Journal of Management*, 35(6), 1404–1427.

Hirschman, A. O. (1970). *Exit, Voice, and Loyalty: Responses to Decline in Firms, Organizations, and States* (Vol. 25). Cambridge, MA: Harvard University Press.

Hoskisson, R. E., Hitt, M. A., Johnson, R. A., and Grossman, W. (2002). Conflicting voices: The effects of institutional ownership heterogeneity and internal governance on corporate innovation strategies. *Academy of Management Journal*, 45(4), 697–716.

Huxham, C. and Vangen, S. (2005). *Managing to Collaborate: The Theory and Practice of Collaborative Advantage*. Abingdon, UK: Routledge.

Isett, K. R., Mergel, I. A., LeRoux, K., Mischen, P. A., and Rethemeyer, R. K. (2011). Networks in public administration scholarship: Understanding where we are and where we need to go. *Journal of Public Administration Research and Theory*, 21(suppl. 1), i157–i173.

Jackman, S. (2009). *Bayesian Analysis for the Social Sciences* (Vol. 846). Hoboken, NJ: John Wiley.

Jensen, M. C. and Meckling, W. H. (1976). Theory of the firm: Managerial behavior, agency costs and ownership structure. *Journal of Financial Economics*, 3(4), 305–360.

John, K. and Senbet, L. W. (1998). Corporate governance and board effectiveness. *Journal of Banking & Finance*, 22(4), 371–403.

Kale, P., Dyer, J. H., and Singh, H. (2002). Alliance capability, stock market response, and long-term alliance success: The role of the alliance function. *Strategic Management Journal*, 23(8), 747–767.

Kang, J. K. and Shivdasani, A. (1995). Firm performance, corporate governance, and top executive turnover in Japan. *Journal of Financial Economics*, 38(1), 29–58.

Kesner, I. F. and Sebora, T. C. (1994). Executive succession: Past, present and future. *Journal of Management*, 20(2), 327–372.

Kiewiet, D. R. and McCubbins, M. D. (1991). *The Logic of Delegation*. Chicago, IL: University of Chicago Press.

Kickert, W. J., Klijn, E. H., and Koppenjan, J. F., eds. (1997). *Managing Complex Networks: Strategies for the Public Sector*. Thousand Oaks, CA: Sage.

Kille, K. (2006). *From Manager to Visionary: The Secretary-General of the United Nations*. New York, NY: Springer.

Klijn, E. H. (2004). *Managing Uncertainties in Networks* London: Routledge.

Koremenos, B., Lipson, C. and Snidal, D. (2001) Rational design: Looking back to move forward. *International Organization*, 55(4), 1051–1082.

Kraske, J., Becker, W. H., Diamond, W., and Galambos, L., eds. (1996). *Bankers With a Mission: The Presidents of the World Bank, 1946–91*. Washington, DC: World Bank Publications.

La Porta, R., Lopez-de-Silanes, F., and Shleifer, A. (1999). Corporate ownership around the world. *The Journal of Finance*, 54(2), 471–517.

Leech, D. and Leahy, J. (1991). Ownership structure, control type classifications and the performance of large British companies. *The Economic Journal*, 101(409), 1418–1437.

Levine, R. (2004). *The Corporate Governance of Banks: A Concise Discussion of Concepts and Evidence*. Washington, DC: World Bank Publications.

Locke, E. A. and G. P. Latham. (2002). Building a practically useful theory of goal setting and task motivation: A 35-year odyssey. *American Psychologist*, 57(9), 705–717.

Long, R. J. (1980). Job attitudes and organizational performance under employee ownership. *Academy of Management Journal*, 23(4), 726–737.

Lorange, P. (1980) *Corporate Planning: An Executive Viewpoint*. Englewood Cliffs, NJ: Prentice Hall.

Lindblom, C. (1959). The science of muddling through. *Public Administration Review*, 19(2), 79–88.

Lyne, M. M., Nielson, D. L., and Tierney, M. J. (2006). Who delegates? Alternative models of principals in development aid. In Hawkins, D. G., Lake, D. A.,

Nielson, D. L., and Tierney, M. J., eds., *Delegation and Agency in International Organizations*. Cambridge, UK: Cambridge University Press, 44.

Macey, J. R. and O'Hara, M. (2003). The corporate governance of banks. *Economic Policy Review*, 9(1), 91–107.

Marshall, M. G. and Jaggers, K. (2002). *Polity IV Project: Political Regime Characteristics and Transitions, 1800–2002: Dataset Users' Manual*. Maryland, MD: University of Maryland.

McNulty, T. and Pettigrew, A. (1999). Strategists on the board. *Organization Studies*, 20(1), 47–74.

Mayer, R. C., Davis, J. H., and Schoorman, F. D. (1995). An integrative model of organizational trust. *Academy of Management Review*, 20(3), 709–734.

Meyer, J. W., and Rowan, B. (1977). Institutionalized organizations: Formal structure as myth and ceremony. *American Journal of Sociology*, 83(2), 340–363.

Miles, R. and Snow, C. (1978) *Organizational strategy, structure and process*. New York, NY: McGraw-Hill.

Miller, D., Kets de Vries, M. F. , and Toulouse, J. M. (1982). Top executive locus of control and its relationship to strategy-making, structure, and environment. *Academy of Management Journal*, 25(2), 237–253.

Mintzberg, H. (1973). Strategy-making in three modes. *California Management Review*, 16(2), 44–53.

Mintzberg, H. (1993). *Structure in Fives: Designing Effective Organizations*. Englewood Cliffs, NJ: Prentice Hall.

Misangyi, V. F., Greckhamer, T., Furnari, S., Fiss, P. C., Crilly, D., and Aguilera, R. V. (2017). Embracing causal complexity: The emergence of a neo-configurational perspective. *Journal of Management*, 43(1), 255–282.

Mitchell, W. (1994). The dynamics of evolving markets: The effects of business sales and age on dissolutions and divestitures. *Administrative Science Quarterly*, 39(4), 575–602.

Mitchell, R. K., Agle, B. R., and Wood, D. J. (1997). Toward a theory of stakeholder identification and salience: Defining the principle of who and what really counts. *Academy of Management Review*, 22(4), 853–886.

Mitrany, D. (1948). The functional approach to world organization. *International Affairs (Royal Institute of International Affairs 1944–)*, 24(3), 350–363.

Mizruchi, M. S. (1983). Who controls whom? An examination of the relation between management and boards of directors in large American corporations. *Academy of Management Review*, 8(3), 426–435.

Mohr, J. and Spekman, R. (1994). Characteristics of partnership success: Partnership attributes, communication behavior, and conflict resolution techniques. *Strategic Management Journal*, 15(2), 135–152.

Müller-Seitz, G. (2012). Leadership in interorganizational networks: A literature review and suggestions for future research. *International Journal of Management Reviews*, 14(4), 428–443.

Ness, G. D. and Brechin, S. R. (1988). Bridging the gap: International organizations as organizations. *International Organization*, 42(2), 245–273.

Nicholson, G. J. and Kiel, G. C. (2007). Can directors impact performance? A case-based test of three theories of corporate governance. *Corporate Governance: An International Review*, 15(4), 585–608.

Nielson, D. L. and Tierney, M. J. (2003). Delegation to international organizations: Agency theory and World Bank environmental reform. *International Organization*, 57(2), 241–276.

Northouse, P. G. (2010). *Authentic Leadership. Leadership Theory and Practice* (5th ed.). Los Angeles, CA: Sage, 205–239.

Nye Jr.,J. S. (2013). *Presidential Leadership and the Creation of the American Era*. Princeton, NJ: Princeton University Press.

Ocasio, W. and Kim, H. (1999). The circulation of corporate control: Selection of functional backgrounds of new CEOs in large US manufacturing firms, 1981–1992. *Administrative Science Quarterly*, 44(3), 532–562.

Oesterle, M. J., Richta, H. N., and Fisch, J. H. (2013). The influence of ownership structure on internationalization. *International Business Review*, 22(1), 187–201.

Olson, M. (1965). *The Logic of Collective Action: Public Goods and the Theory of Groups*. Cambridge, MA: Harvard University Press.

Ospina, S. M. and Saz-Carranza, A. (2010). Paradox and collaboration in network management. *Administration & Society*, 42(4), 404–440.

Parente, T. C. and Federo, R. (2019). Qualitative comparative analysis: Justifying a neo-configurational approach in management research. *RAUSP Management Journal*, 54(4), 399–412.

Pevehouse, J., Nordstrom, T., and Warnke, K. (2004). The Correlates of War 2 international governmental organizations data version 2.0. *Conflict Management and Peace Science*, 21(2), 101–119.

Peng, M. W., Tan, J., and Tong, T. W. (2004). Ownership types and strategic groups in an emerging economy. *Journal of Management Studies*, 41(7), 1105–1129.

Pfeffer, J. and Salancik, G. R. (1978). *The External Control of Organizations: A Resource-Dependence Perspective*. Redwood City, CA: Stanford University Press.

Phan, P. H., Siegel, D. S., and Wright, M. (2005). Science parks and incubators: Observations, synthesis and future research. *Journal of Business Venturing*, 20(2), 165–182.

Pierce, J. L. and Delbecq, A. L. (1977). Organization structure, individual attitudes and innovation. *Academy of Management Review*, 2(1), 27–37.

Pierce, J. L., Rubenfeld, S. A., and Morgan, S. (1991). Employee ownership: A conceptual model of process and effects. *Academy of Management Review*, 16(1), 121–144.

Plummer, M. (2013). rjags: Bayesian graphical models using MCMC. *R package version*, 3(10).

Porta, R. L., Lopez-de-Silanes, F., Shleifer, A., and Vishny, R. W. (1998). Law and finance. *Journal of Political Economy*, 106(6), 1113–1155.

Provan, K. G. and Kenis, P. (2008). Modes of network governance: Structure, management, and effectiveness. *Journal of Public Administration Research and Theory*, 18(2), 229–252.

Pugh, D. S., Hickson, D. J., Hinings, C. R., and Turner, C. (1968). Dimensions of organization structure. *Administrative Science Quarterly*, 13, 65–105.

Quinn, J. B. (1980). *Strategies for Change: Logical Incrementalism.* Homewood, IL: Richard D. Irwin.

Richard, P. J., Devinney, T. M., Yip, G. S., and Johnson, G. (2009) Measuring organizational performance: Towards methodological best practice. *Journal of Management*, 35(3), 718–804.

Ruggie, J. G. (1982). International regimes, transactions, and change: Embedded liberalism in the postwar economic order. *International Organization*, 36(2), 379–415.

Rutherford, A. and Lozano, J. (2018). Top management turnover: The role of governing board structures. *Public Administration Review*, 78(1), 104–115.

Salancik, G. R. and Pfeffer, J. (1974). The bases and use of power in organizational decision-making: The case of a university. *Administrative Science Quarterly*, 19(4), 453–473.

Saz-Carranza, A. (2012). *Uniting Diverse Organizations: Managing Goal-Oriented Advocacy Networks*. Abingdon, UK: Routledge.

Saz-Carranza, A. (2015). Agents as brokers: Leadership in multilateral organizations. *Global Policy*, 6(3), 277–289.

Saz-Carranza, A., Albareda, A., and Federo, R. (2020). Network tasks and accountability: A configurational analysis of EU regulatory networks. *Public Administration*, 98(2): 480–497.

Saz-Carranza, A., Fernandez-i-Marin, X., Federo, R., and Losada, C. (2018). Balancing effectiveness and control in global intergovernmental organizations. In *Academy of Management Proceedings* 2018(1). Briarcliff Manor, NY: Academy of Management, p. 12778.

Schemeil, Y. (2013). Bringing international organization in: Global institutions as adaptive hybrids. *Organization Studies*, 34(2), 219–252.

Sebora, T. C. and Kesner, I. F. (1996). The CEO selection decision process: Bounded rationality and decision component ordering. *Journal of Multi-Criteria Decision Analysis*, 5(3), 183–194.

Shaffer, G. (2015). How the World Trade Organization shapes regulatory governance. *Regulation & Governance*, 9(1), 1–15.

Silvia, C. and McGuire, M. (2010). Leading public sector networks: An empirical examination of integrative leadership behaviors. *The Leadership Quarterly*, 21(2), 264–277.

Simmons, B. (2008). International law and international relations. In Whittington, K. E., Kelemen, R. D., and Caldeira, G. A., eds., *The Oxford Handbook of Law and Politics* (187–208). Oxford, UK: Oxford University Press.

Simon, H. A. (1948). *The Sciences of the Artificial*. Cambridge, MA: MIT Press.

Stuart, T. E. and Podolny, J. M. (1996). Local search and the evolution of technological capabilities. *Strategic Management Journal*, 17(S1), 21–38.

Suchman, M. C. (1995). Managing legitimacy: Strategic and institutional approaches. *Academy of Management Review*, 20(3), 571–610.

Sundaramurthy, C. and Lewis, M. (2003). Control and collaboration: Paradoxes of governance. *Academy of Management Review*, 28(3), 397–415.

Steijn, B. and Klijn, E. (2008). The impact of network management in governance networks. *Public Administration*, 88, 1–21.

Stone, R. (2013). Informal governance in international organizations: Introduction to the special issue. *The Review of International Organizations*, 8(2), 121–136.

Suchman, M. C. (1995). Managing legitimacy: Strategic and institutional approaches. *Academy of Management Review*, 20(3), 571–610.

Sur, S., Lvina, E., and Magnan, M. (2013). Why do boards differ? Because owners do: Assessing ownership impact on board composition. *Corporate Governance: An International Review*, 21(4), 373–389.

Tallberg, J. (2004). The power of the presidency: Brokerage, efficiency and distribution in EU negotiations. *JCMS: Journal of Common Market Studies*, 42(5), 999–1022.

Tallberg, J. (2010). The power of the chair: Formal leadership in international cooperation. *International Studies Quarterly*, 54(1), 241–265.

Tallberg, J. and Zürn, M. (2019). The legitimacy and legitimation of international organizations: Introduction and framework. *The Review of International Organizations*, 14(4), 581–606.

Team, R. C. (2013). *R: A language and environment for statistical computing.* http://cran.univ-paris1.fr/web/packages/dplR/vignettes/intro-dplR.pdf.

Teece, D. J., Pisano, G., and Shuen, A. (1997). Dynamic capabilities and strategic management. *Strategic Management Journal*, 18(7), 509–533.

Van den Berghe, L. A. and Levrau, A. (2004). Evaluating boards of directors: What constitutes a good corporate board? *Corporate Governance: An International Review*, 12(4), 461–478.

Volgy, T. J., Fausett, E., Grant, K. and Rodgers, S. (2008). Identifying formal intergovernmental organizations. *Journal of Peace Research*, 45(6), 837–850.

Walker, R. M., Brewer, G. A., Bozeman, B., Moon, M. J., and Wu, J. (2013). An experimental assessment of public ownership and performance. *Public Management Review*, 15(8), 1208–1228.

Westphal, J. D. (1999). Collaboration in the boardroom: Behavioral and performance consequences of CEO-board social ties. *Academy of Management Journal*, 42(1), 7–24.

Westphal, J. D. and Fredrickson, J. W. (2001). Who directs strategic change? Director experience, the selection of new CEOs, and change in corporate strategy. *Strategic Management Journal*, 22(12), 1113–1137.

Williamson, O. E. (1979). Transaction-cost economics: The governance of contractual relations. *The Journal of Law and Economics*, 22(2), 233–261.

Young, M. N., Peng, M. W., Ahlstrom, D., Bruton, G. D., and Jiang, Y. (2008). Corporate governance in emerging economies: A review of the principal–principal perspective. *Journal of Management Studies*, 45(1), 196–220.

Zajac, E. J. (1990). CEO selection, succession, compensation and firm performance: A theoretical integration and empirical analysis. *Strategic Management Journal*, 11(3), 217–230.

Zahra, S. A. and Nielsen, A. P. (2002). Sources of capabilities, integration and technology commercialization. *Strategic Management Journal*, 23(5), 377–398.

Zahra, S. A. and Pearce, J. A. (1989). Boards of directors and corporate financial performance: A review and integrative model. *Journal of Management*, 15(2), 291–334.

Zahra, S. A. and Pearce, J. A. (1990). Determinants of board directors' strategic involvement. *European Management Journal*, 8(2), 164–173.

Zhang, Y. and Rajagopalan, N. (2010). Once an outsider, always an outsider? CEO origin, strategic change, and firm performance. *Strategic Management Journal*, 31(3), 334–346.

Zucker, L. G. (1986). Production of trust: Institutional sources of economic structure, 1840–1920. *Research in Organizational Behavior*, 8, 53–111.

Cambridge Elements ≡

Public and Nonprofit Administration

Andrew Whitford
University of Georgia
Andrew Whitford is Alexander M. Crenshaw Professor of Public Policy in the School of Public and International Affairs at the University of Georgia. His research centers on strategy and innovation in public policy and organization studies.

Robert Christensen
Brigham Young University
Robert Christensen is professor and George Romney Research Fellow in the Marriott School at Brigham Young University. His research focuses on prosocial and antisocial behaviors and attitudes in public and nonprofit organizations.

About the Series
The foundation of this series are cutting-edge contributions on emerging topics and definitive reviews of keystone topics in public and nonprofit administration, especially those that lack longer treatment in textbook or other formats. Among keystone topics of interest for scholars and practitioners of public and nonprofit administration, it covers public management, public budgeting and finance, nonprofit studies, and the interstitial space between the public and nonprofit sectors, along with theoretical and methodological contributions, including quantitative, qualitative and mixed-methods pieces.

The Public Management Research Association
The Public Management Research Association improves public governance by advancing research on public organizations, strengthening links among interdisciplinary scholars, and furthering professional and academic opportunities in public management.

Cambridge Elements $\equiv$

Public and Nonprofit Administration

Elements in the Series

Motivating Public Employees
Marc Esteve and Christian Schuster

Organizational Obliviousness: Entrenched Resistance to Gender Integration in the Military
Alesha Doan and Shannon Portillo

Partnerships that Last: Identifying the Keys to Resilient Collaboration
Heather Getha-Taylor

Behavioral Public Performance: How People Make Sense of Government Metrics
Oliver James, Donald P. Moynihan, Asmus Leth Olsen and Gregg G. Van Ryzin

Redefining Development: Resolving Complex Challenges in Developing Countries
Jessica Kritz

Gender, Risk and Leadership: The Glass Cliff in Public Service Careers
Leisha DeHart-Davis, Deneen Hatmaker, Kim Nelson, Sanjay K. Pandey,
Sheela Pandey and Amy Smith

Institutional Memory as Storytelling: How Networked Government Remembers
Jack Corbett, Dennis Christian Grube, Heather Caroline Lovell and Rodney
James Scott

How Local Governments Govern Culture War Conflicts
Mark Chou and Rachel Busbridge

Global Climate Governance
David Coen, Julia Kreienkamp and Tom Pegram

Management and Governance of Intergovernmental Organizations
Ryan Federo, Angel Saz-Carranza and Marc Esteve

A full series listing is available at: www.cambridge.org/EPNP

Printed in the United States
By Bookmasters